||| || | ||||||||| ||| ||||| |||
I0155605

Shattered Reflections

Finding Confidence in the Cracks, Purpose in the Pieces, and Clarity to Write Your Own Story

Talie Rowe

Platypus Publishing

Disclaimer:

This book and its accompanying materials are for informational and educational purposes only. They are not intended to diagnose, treat, cure, or prevent any emotional, mental, or medical condition. The author is not a licensed therapist, counselor, psychologist, or medical professional. Nothing in this book or its related resources should be considered professional advice.

Always seek the guidance of a qualified mental health or medical professional if you have any questions regarding your well-being. Never disregard professional advice or delay seeking it because of something you have read here.

Your use of this material is voluntary, and the author assumes no responsibility for any outcomes that may result.

Shattered Reflections
© 2025 Talie Rowe
All rights reserved.

No part of this book may be reproduced, distributed, or transmitted in any form or by any means, including photocopying, recording, or other electronic or mechanical methods, without the prior written permission of the author, except for brief quotations used in reviews or articles.

ISBN: 978-1-968253-65-3
First Edition

Author: Talie Rowe
Website: journeybegins.net

For my mother

"All that I am, or hope to be, I owe to my angel mother." — Abraham Lincoln

And my big brothers

"They are my twin pillars, without whom I could not stand..." — Rory Gilmore

Your constant thread of love and strength is woven through every season of my life.

· ♥ · ♥ · ♥ · ♥ · ♥ ·

Contents

Introduction

THE MIRROR WAS LYING

Ever felt like everyone else got the manual, and you're just winging it?

To be fair, my life wasn't exactly tragic. I've always had a loving family and supportive friends. I've always had food on the table, a home to call my own, a job to go to, and a car to get me there. Most importantly, I was never involved in a love triangle with mythical creatures, so things could've been worse. By all accounts, I should've felt content, but still, something was missing. There was this ache I couldn't name, like I was living near my life, not in it. Like I was checking all the boxes but somehow missing the point.

That kind of confusion isn't loud; it hums soft and steady until one day you realize, you're playing a role you never chose. I was trying to be what everyone else needed: strong, put-together, low-maintenance, but never actually free to be me. Honestly? I didn't even know who "me" was. I thought confidence was the formula: work harder, look better, pray more, heal faster. But the harder I tried, the more disoriented I felt, like staring into a funhouse mirror. More on that in a bit...

So, Why This Book?

For years, I felt like a stranger in my own skin, wondering, *"Is this really all there is to me?"* If you've ever stared at your reflection and thought, "If I could fix myself, maybe I'd finally feel worthy," you're not alone.

This is for the people-pleasers, the overthinkers, the quiet achievers, the ones who look "fine" on the outside but feel like they're drowning inside. Maybe you can relate. You've tried it all: books, journaling, affirmations, and somehow still feel lost. You want to believe things can change, but it feels like that kind of healing is reserved for *other* people.

I've been there and want you to know that breaking free is possible. Just keep in mind, this isn't about getting it all right. It's about finding your way back to the person you were created to be.

Here's Some of What We'll Explore Together:

• How your past shaped your self-image and how to start rewriting it.

• How to silence the inner critic and speak to yourself with truth and compassion.

• How fear, perfectionism, and people-pleasing keep you stuck.

• How to stop chasing worth through achievements, approval, or comparison.

• How to move forward with purpose and peace, while the path unfolds.

This is the kind of insight I wish I had back when I mistook silent struggle for strength and wore self-doubt like armor. If that sounds familiar, take heart. Those cracks are often where confidence and clarity start to break through.

You May Be Wondering What I Know...

No, I'm not an expert with letters behind my name. I'm just a woman who stayed in self-doubt too long before finally saying, "Enough." Besides, this book isn't about having all the answers because honestly, I don't. What I do have is a story. It's messy and real, filled with hard-earned lessons and a deep belief that change is possible even when it doesn't look Pinterest-perfect.

One More Thing Before We Start...

You'll see a few mentions of faith in this book, not because I'm trying to convert you, but because my relationship with God is part of my story, just like fear, anxiety, awkward oversharing, and Netflix binges. If I tell my story, I must tell it all...

That said, if the word "God" feels right to you, beautiful. If not, that's okay too. My faith is central to my story, but your beliefs don't have to be the same as mine. You're welcome here, just as you are. Take a deep breath. There's no pressure, only space to grow through tiny shifts, honest reflection, and a few good laughs.

Welcome to the journey...

Part 1

Breaking the Cycle of Self-Doubt

"You can't heal what you won't face."

———————◆O◆———————

It's time to dig up the lies, sit with the hard stuff, and uncover the roots of your self-doubt. This is where we stop just getting by and start truly seeing ourselves, flaws and all. This is the beginning of real healing.

Chapter 0

THE FIRST LOOK IN THE MIRROR

Chapter 0. Weird? Maybe. But so am I. Honestly, I think the best people are, so it works.

Before we dive into healing, unlearning, and rebuilding, I want to tell you how everything changed for me and what made me stop and ask, "Wait...how did I end up here?" I called this *Chapter 0* because it came before all the steps, strategies, and soul-searching you'll find in the pages ahead. Without it, there would be no Chapter 1, and that deserves a little credit.

So, let's get into it...

I didn't always have a name for it—that vague sense that something was off. I could ace a test, land a compliment, and still feel like a fraud. My reflection felt less like a face and more like a weight pressing on my chest, carrying all the expectations, shame, and self-judgment I'd been holding onto. The feeling lingered, faithful as a shadow. Eventually, I gave it a name: *The Funhouse Mirror.*

You've seen carnival mirrors, right? The ones that stretch your body like taffy or squash you into a cartoon blob? That's how my reflection felt, inside and out. It was like things I couldn't see had bent my entire self-image out of shape. Years of subtle neglect, compliments with conditions, and a culture constantly whispering, "You're not enough."

I was trying to build a life based on twisted feedback. When you spend years staring at a warped mirror, sooner or later you start to believe it. That's the thing about funhouses, they're designed to confuse you. They want you to lose your sense of direction. They're built for distortion, not clarity.

> *"The mirror shows your reflection, but only truth reveals your identity."*

SO, WHAT'S IN A NAME? (A LOT, APPARENTLY)

I started calling it the Funhouse Mirror after watching a scene from one of my favorite shows, set in my favorite fictional town with my favorite TV mom. She made a throwaway joke about a funhouse mirror that always makes me laugh, but that day, it felt different. I could picture myself standing before one—stretched, distorted, unrecognizable. That image reflected exactly how I felt inside, like I was being crushed by something invisible. Naming it helped. It gave me something to point to other than myself.

Before, when my thoughts spiraled, it was hard to talk myself down. But once that distorted reflection became a symbol, I could recognize what was happening. That mental picture became my signal: Okay, time to shift. Time to redirect. Time to do something different.

Now I catch it much sooner. I feel my energy shift and think, *"Wait... is that circus music? Nope, not today."* And if someone tries to drag me into emotional chaos, I tell myself, *"Sorry, not going to the carnival,"* and walk away. I know it might sound silly, but if metaphorical mirrors and imaginary carnivals help me protect my peace, I'm good with that.

Before I learned more about myself, there were moments I couldn't tell when I was in the funhouse; I knew something felt...off. Well, more specifically, I felt downright miserable. Not the "Ugh, I need a nap" miserable, I'm talking soul-deep, *"How did I end up here?"* miserable.

Then, during another doom scrolling session, I heard someone say: "No one is coming to save you...No one is coming to push you...It's all up to YOU."

Slap in the face? Yes.

Much-needed reality check? Also, yes.

That moment didn't fix everything, but it made me realize that waiting for something (or someone) to fix my life was another way I kept handing over my power. If my life were to get better, I had to be the one to do it. Which sounds great, unless you're trying to overhaul your entire life while paralyzed by self-doubt and terrified of failing. Fun times, huh?

So I broke Project Overhaul into bite-sized pieces. I found a therapist and began reconnecting with something bigger than myself. For me, that's God. I discovered a pastor I liked on YouTube, swapped music for motivational podcasts, and buried myself in a mountain of personal growth and faith-based books. The messages I absorbed reminded me that fear, not failure, was holding me back. They challenged my excuses, encouraged me to dream again, and showed me that growth was possible. Slowly, things started to shift, and I felt stronger.

I heard quotes that stuck with me, like:

- "You are fearfully and wonderfully made." (Psalm 139:14 NIV)

- "If my mind can conceive it, and my heart can believe it, then I can achieve it." (attributed to Muhammad Ali)

- "If you always do what you've always done, you'll always be where you've always been." (anonymous)

Those words made me confront what I'd been avoiding: I wasn't simply stuck in park, I was trapped in a mindset shaped by low self-worth. The idea that I could have more or be more was impossible to believe. I knew my sense of worth needed work, and my confidence was fragile, but I hadn't grasped how deeply that ran or how much it was quietly driving my decisions behind the scenes.

Just when I thought I'd had my biggest revelation, my therapist hit me with the phrase "daddy issues." *Cue the longest eye roll of my life.* It was hard to hear but necessary, because naming the root cause of my issues wasn't just therapeutic—it was clarifying. The dots started to connect, and once I could name the problem, I could finally start fighting back. (Metaphorically, of course. I'm not out here throwing hands with my past.)

How Low Self-Worth Quietly Runs the Show

Naming it helped me see the distortion, but healing meant tracing it back to the source. Beneath every twisted thought and self-sabotaging choice was something deeper, a small fracture at the foundation. Low self-worth doesn't crash into your life like thunder; it seeps in like a leak, subtle and steady. It reshapes how you speak to yourself, how you show up, and what you tolerate. It influences your relationships, mental health, decisions, and even what you believe you deserve. How you see yourself determines how you move through the world, which matters.

When you believe something negative about yourself, your brain starts collecting "evidence" to prove it. (Psychologists call this confirmation bias: it reinforces whatever story you've been telling yourself, even if it's not true.) The longer that voice whispers, "You're not good enough," the more convincing it sounds. In time, it stops feeling like insecurity and starts sounding like a fact. That mindset can lead to anxiety, depression, people-pleasing, and self-sabotage. It shrinks your world until life feels smaller than what you were made for. I know, because I've lived it.

I've learned that healing doesn't start when you love yourself; it starts when you stop lying to yourself. When you stop pretending you're fine, stop shrinking to be accepted, and face the parts of you that hurt instead of hiding them. It's uncomfortable at first, like turning on the light in a room you've avoided for years, but that's where truth lives. And truth is what sets you free. Real healing begins not in the mirror, but in the soul. Only then can self-love become deep, real, and lasting. But first, you have to confront the beliefs holding you hostage.

FROM FOG TO FOCUS

They say that your beliefs shape your identity, and your identity shapes your actions. That meant I had to stop believing I was stuck, unworthy, or "not good enough," and start believing I was capable, valuable, and chosen. I had to trust there was a purpose for my life and I wasn't too late to find it. The more I leaned into that, the more things started to shift.

When you see yourself clearly, everything else starts coming into focus.

✔ Your dreams don't feel silly; they feel sacred.

✔ Your past no longer defines you; it shapes you.

✔ Your struggles start to look less like roadblocks and more like stepping stones.

Clarity doesn't come from having all the answers but from the courage to face what's true right now. I used to think that if I could just figure out my purpose, the path would magically appear. But purpose isn't the starting point, understanding is. The moment I began to see myself clearly, the maze gave way to direction.

WHAT THEY DIDN'T SEE BEHIND THE SMILE

The more I learned about myself, the clearer it became: my therapist was right... I did have "daddy issues." I resisted the idea because I hate that term; it's so cliché and it puts all the shame on the child. These days, I call it a father wound, a phrase I first heard in a book and immediately connected with because it lifts the weight I was never meant to carry.

Still, acknowledging it was like unlocking a door I didn't know I'd been pounding on. It revealed the missing piece, the wound etched into me before I even had a chance to understand.

My father was gone before I took my first breath. He returned when I was a preteen, but the damage was done. He had a new family and kids he adored. Me? I was there—present, but not chosen. Loved, maybe. But love you can't feel is like a song never heard.

My mom raised me alone, pouring everything she had into giving me a good life. She is my rock, my avenger, my everything. I also have two big brothers whose love is unwavering, and I adore them just the same. Together, the three of them are my safe place, supported by a wider circle of family never far behind. Yet even love that steady couldn't quiet the lie I carried: I wasn't enough.

I was a shadow my father could never outrun, and I felt like I ruined his life just by being born. That narrative looped like a soundtrack in my head for years. It didn't take long before those thoughts stopped hiding in the background and started calling the shots. They became the quiet script behind every decision, the reason I settled for less, smiled through disappointment, and mistook crumbs for connection.

I took jobs I didn't like because I believed I couldn't do better. I stayed in relationships with emotionally unavailable men because I thought that was all I could get. All I wanted was to be chosen, or in the immortal words of my girl Meredith Grey: "Pick me. Choose me. Love me." But deep down, I already knew no one would.

I carried that ache for years. I tried to outrun it with achievements, approval, distractions—anything. But no matter how far I ran, that old feeling always found me. I didn't know how to fix it. I just knew I couldn't keep living like this. Something had to give. Then, in the middle of an ordinary conversation, something changed.

A PAUSE. A QUESTION. A SPARK

One day, I was venting to my best friend about how unhappy I was. I was overanalyzing everything (as usual), and when she asked why I was being so indecisive, I told her I was scared to fail. She paused, then said, "I don't understand that. I've never seen you fail at anything." That stopped me cold, because she was right. Sure, I wasn't taking wild risks, but when I did decide on something, I usually succeeded. It made me pause and think: *Wait, am I secretly a badass and didn't know it?*

Her words hit harder than I expected—they poked a hole in the story I'd been telling myself for years. Maybe I wasn't incapable. Maybe I'd just been conditioned to doubt myself.

Later, I came across this quote: "If you've never failed, you've never tried." And boom, ego deflated. Even my so-called "successes" came from playing it safe. But the more I learned about failure, the more I realized it wasn't something to avoid, it was something to redefine.

These quotes helped reshape my thinking:

- "Failure is simply the opportunity to begin again, this time more intelligently." —Henry Ford

- "Only those who dare to fail greatly can ever achieve greatly." —Robert F. Kennedy

- "You have to fail in order to practice being brave." —Mary Tyler Moore

- "The greatest teacher, failure is." —Yoda (Tiny Jedi, giant mic drop)

Those words felt like tiny permission slips, proof that failure wasn't fatal and might even be necessary. My best friend sparked it, the quotes fueled it, and together they handed me what I didn't realize I'd been missing: clarity.

BEEN THERE, READ THAT, STILL CONFUSED

Having clarity in my head was one thing; living it out was another. Even with new insights, I still found myself stuck in old patterns, wondering why all the "right" tools weren't working. The books? Read. The journals? Filled. The affirmations? Performed in my best Oprah voice. And still, I felt stuck.

For a while, all those tools felt like empty rituals. I was doing the "work," but deep down, I didn't believe it could change anything—not for me, anyway. And journaling felt especially ridiculous. Who wants to stare at their deepest fears and messiest thoughts in black and white? It all felt like homework for a class I wasn't prepared for. I kept waiting for a big breakthrough, some magic "aha" moment that would finally make it click, but life isn't a montage, and healing doesn't happen to background music.

But here's what I found: those ramblings eventually became revelations. And over time, those revelations led to healing. And now a book. Hopefully that's encouraging. If not, I'm still here to tell you—don't give up.

Maybe it's not about trying harder; maybe it's about shifting how you try. Journal outside. Say your affirmations in the mirror. Pray as you walk. Write a letter to your future self. Mix the old with the new and create a rhythm that works for you.

Most importantly, remember that healing doesn't come with fireworks. Sometimes it's quiet. Sometimes it's boring, but that doesn't mean it's not working. It takes time to sink in, but when it does, everything changes.

HEALING, MY WAY

I didn't have one big breakthrough. Small pivots and quiet choices born of hope and exhaustion slowly reshaped my life.

Over time, here's what began to change:

- I stopped waiting to "feel ready" and started moving.

- I stopped chasing perfection and trusted that progress was enough.

- I stopped trying to go it alone and started inviting God into the process, not as an idea, but as my anchor.

Journaling revealed the patterns, and books gave me the language. But action carried me forward, each small choice stacking into a quiet transformation. The result? A then vs. now testimony of grace and growth.

Then, I believed I wasn't enough.

Now, I know I am.

Then, I lived for other people's approval.

Now, I live with clarity, not comparison.

It came in pieces, slowly, sometimes painfully. But I kept going, and my story began to take shape step by step.

And now, here's your invitation to see yourself clearly, rewrite your story, and rebuild from the inside out... because you're worth it.

Chapter 1

UNCOVERING WHAT'S HOLDING YOU BACK

Let's start with a common mix-up: self-worth and confidence are not the same thing.

Confidence is knowing you can rise to the challenge because you trust your skills and abilities. You might feel it when giving a presentation or cooking a killer Sunday dinner because you've done it before and know you can handle it.

Self-worth, though? That's something else entirely. It's about who you believe you are at your core—your value before achievements, applause, or approval.

Here's where it gets tricky: you can be confident in what you do and still have low self-worth. You can look successful on paper, get applause at work, and still feel like you're not enough. That's because we build confidence by doing. But self-worth runs beneath all that; it's shaped by what we believe about ourselves, whether true or not. Hold on to false beliefs long enough, and they start to feel normal. And once they do, the warped reflection becomes your reality.

But those beliefs don't appear out of nowhere. Somewhere along the way, you may have been told (or shown) that you weren't smart enough, pretty enough, talented enough, or _____ (insert your insecurity). And if you don't challenge those lies, you carry them around, and they start calling the shots. They keep you playing small, convincing you to settle.

They stop you from applying, speaking up, setting boundaries, or trying new things. So know this: the goal isn't to slap a confidence sticker on top of shaky self-worth. It's healing the parts of you that were never meant to carry those lies in the first place.

> *"You can't fix what you won't face."*

THE LIES THAT LIVED RENT-FREE IN MY HEAD

Over the years, I've had some serious internal trash talk on repeat. Here are a few of my greatest hits:

- "You'll never be successful because you're not talented enough."

- "You're not smart enough."

- "You're not pretty enough, sexy enough, skinny enough."

- "No guy will ever love you."

Yup, these are the classics, and depending on the day, they still try to make a comeback. Each was born from my Funhouse

Mirror, where flaws loomed larger, insecurities screamed louder, and anything good shrank until it was nearly gone.

Growth taught me that these thoughts were rooted in comparison. I compared myself to my dad's other kids—the chosen ones. I compared myself to my tiny, gorgeous cousins (I tower over them like a friendly giant), and to my friends, who were confident, accomplished, and somehow always put together. Then social media came in like a wrecking ball. Suddenly, I was stacking myself up against women worldwide.

Not to be outdone, a teenage boyfriend once rated me a solid "7", but as "encouragement," added that I'd be a "10" if I had a flat stomach. No wonder my self-worth looked like a clearance toaster—dented, but technically still functional.

After my last toxic relationship (yes, I have a type; we're working on it), I was mentally and emotionally drained. One day, while grumbling to a friend about being single and unlovable, she stopped me and said, "There are a million people who love you and gravitate toward you. You're funny, kind, and you make people feel better by being around. Just because you haven't found a guy who sees that yet doesn't mean you're not all that and a bag of chips."

I laughed, but that little pep talk planted a seed. It reminded me that I can build deep, lasting friendships with anyone: men, women, young, or old. Truthfully, I'm kind of like a chameleon. So why did I believe I wasn't good enough to be loved romantically? That thought lit a spark of possibility. It didn't erase all the doubt, but made me curious enough to start questioning the script. And sometimes, that's all it takes.

REFRAMING THE NARRATIVE

Reframing is challenging and replacing your thoughts with something more honest and empowering. But it's not easy, especially when lies feel more familiar. Still, once you get the hang of it? Game changer.

Here's how I reframed some of my most persistent lies:

Lie: *"You'll never be successful because you're not talented enough."*

Truth: Talent can be developed, and success looks different for everyone.

Lie: *"You're not smart enough."*

Truth: I may not know everything right now, but I can learn.

Lie: *"You're not pretty enough, sexy enough, skinny enough."*

Truth: I may not fit society's version of "enough," but I'm still worthy as I am.

Lie: *"No guy will ever love you."*

Truth: The right relationship will come at the right time, but my value doesn't begin or end with someone else's ability to see it.

These truths didn't erase years of doubt, but I kept them close. Literally, I wrote them down and read them often. With time, therapy, books, a lot of prayer, and that spark of possibility, I started to feel a change. That spark turned into a small flame...I wasn't healed, but I was *healing*.

THE ORIGINS OF LOW SELF-WORTH

If you're wondering where all those harsh beliefs come from, you're not alone. I can tell you they don't appear overnight like an Amazon Prime delivery. They're planted early and watered over time by the people, places, and situations you've encountered along the way.

For some, it starts in childhood—constant criticism or emotional neglect that makes love feel conditional. For others, it's bullying in school, toxic relationships, or repeated "failures." And of course, comparison culture doesn't help. Everyone's busy curating their highlight reel while you're just trying not to trip over the props backstage.

Even if your story looks different, the effect is often the same. You start believing you're the problem when really, you were just adapting to the environment you were given.

THE WAYS WE DISAPPEAR

Sometimes the funhouse mirror is so subtle you barely notice it. Often, it looks like slowly shrinking yourself to fit someone else's expectations. Other times, it's trading authenticity for approval—bit by bit, decision by decision—until the person staring back at you feels like a stranger.

Here's what that can look like in real life:

- **Self-doubt & overthinking:** second-guessing even the smallest decisions.

- **Perfectionism:** believing that mistakes cancel out everything you've done right.

- **People-pleasing:** saying "yes" when your whole body is screaming "no."

- **Avoidance:** holding back from trying because you're afraid to fail.

- **Settling:** accepting less than you deserve because you've convinced yourself there isn't more for you.

Fun Fact: I never saw the link between perfectionism and low self-worth; now the dots align perfectly. If you're perfect, no one can criticize you. If you don't mess up, you don't give anyone a reason to leave. It's a coping mechanism that will drain you, and the cost certainly adds up.

When Empowerment Isn't Empowering

Sometimes, low self-worth hides behind slogans that sound like wisdom, but not every affirmation sets you free; some only decorate the cage. And here's where it gets extra spicy: those "empowering" lies are really just self-sabotage with good PR.

One of my favorites? "It'll happen if it's meant to be." It sounds nice and feels calming, but for me... it was an escape route, an excuse to avoid effort, risk, or decision-making. It let me dodge responsibility by slapping a faith-flavored sticker on my fear. Yes, trust in timing. Yes, surrender. But also, move your feet.

Of course, not every excuse wears a catchy slogan. Some slip in as everyday lines we tell ourselves to justify staying stuck. My go-to? "I've got a lot going on right now." While it's true that life gets hectic, this was my all-access pass to staying small. Life can be a lot. That doesn't mean you stop growing.

I still catch myself using that one from time to time. When I do, I pause and check in: Am I truly overwhelmed? Or am I scared, insecure, or avoiding something uncomfortable? Usually, it's a combination platter. But awareness is only half the battle. Once you see what's really going on, you can finally deal with it. Remember, you can't defeat a monster until you unmask it. *(Cue Scooby-Doo music.)*

But here's the deal: nothing changes if nothing changes.

To get a different life, I had to stop waiting for my circumstances to change and start changing them myself. That meant calling myself out lovingly yet honestly. It meant continuously choosing growth over comfort, even when I didn't feel ready... especially then.

So, how do you know the difference between what's empowering and what's a dressed-up excuse? Between helpful guidance and hurtful interference? That's where insight earns its keep.

ADVICE OR AUDACITY?

Healing isn't just about changing your mindset; it's also about tuning in to what's true for *you*. Not all advice is wise. And not all wisdom is yours to carry. One of the hardest parts of growth is figuring out which voices deserve your attention. Just because someone loves you doesn't mean their advice is helpful. And just because someone annoys you doesn't mean they're wrong. Wisdom is knowing the difference between what to keep, question, and toss in the trash with last week's leftovers.

My rule? Hear everything, apply selectively. Part of healing is learning to filter, not just your thoughts, but your influences.

I remember venting to my niece about one of those annoying life problems that feels massive but is totally fixable. When I finished, she stared at me and, in her loving yet assertive tone, asked, "Have you even looked into fixing it?" Ouch. But also... fair. I told her I had, it was too expensive, and I didn't want the hassle. She responded, "Well, if it bothers you that much, do something about it. Complaining won't change a thing." After feeling slightly attacked, I caved... and fixed the problem. She was right, and it was money well spent.

However, not all feedback helps; some of it wounds while pretending to be wise. For example: One of my exes—from a relationship best filed under "life lessons"—started with compliments. Then came the suggestions: eat less of this, work out more, dye your hair, do your nails, refresh your wardrobe, etc.

What started as encouragement became a silent message: *"You're not enough as you are."* As time passed, I asked, "If you want to change everything about me, are you even with me?"

He said he was, but he wasn't really—not with me *me*, anyway. He liked the version of me he built in his mind. But sorry, this isn't Build-a-Bea; you can't customize a person to fit your comfort zone.

Now, to be fair, some of the things did stick. Do I still dye my hair? No. Do I wear makeup? Not really. Do I still do my nails? Absolutely! I'm clickity-clacking as we speak. But I realized real growth isn't about changing to meet other people's expectations. It's about learning which voices deserve a seat at your table and which ones you can kindly show the door.

FROM AWARENESS TO AWAKENING

By now, I hope you're starting to see how the Funhouse Mirror distorts reality, but what about the voice echoing back from inside it, commenting on everything you do? The one that questions your worth, critiques your choices, and whispers doubts when no one else is around.

Up next: Time to face that inner voice, call out its lies, and replace them with a better story.

Chapter 2

REWRITING YOUR INNER DIALOGUE

You know that nagging voice that loves to remind you of every mistake, flaw, and possible way you might fail? Yeah, that's your inner critic and if left unchecked it'll become the loudest voice in the room. The inner critic is a mental bully. It feeds off your fears, insecurities, and self-doubt. It holds you hostage, making you afraid to step outside your comfort zone.

Like any good funhouse mirror, the critic doesn't show you what's real. It stretches your smallest doubts into full-blown insecurities faster than you can say, "Maybe I *am* the problem." Then it twists passing thoughts into bold-faced lies about who you are. The worst part? Half the time, you don't even realize it's happening. It often sounds like your own voice—smart, logical, convincing—and the more you listen, the more believable it becomes.

To start fighting back, you must know what you're up against. Not just the voice itself, but the stories it tells, the way it shows up, and how it tries to keep you small. Because once you recognize the trick, it loses its power. That's where healing begins.

Ask yourself:

- What does my inner critic say on repeat?

- When does it show up the loudest?

  - After a mistake?

  - When I'm about to try something new?

- What tactics does it use to keep me small?

- How does my body react when my inner critic starts talking?

  - Tight chest, racing thoughts, sudden urge to shut down or overwork?

Recognizing your inner critic's voice is the first step to reclaiming your power. But remember, it isn't always loud or cruel. Sometimes it shows up as overworking, overthinking, or over-pleasing. Why? Because underneath those habits are hidden beliefs like:

"I'm only valuable when I'm productive."

"I have to get it right or I'll mess everything up."

"If I don't make everyone happy, I'm not enough."

It's still the critic, quieter maybe, but no less relentless. And once you see how it operates, you stop confusing it with truth.

LOOKING FINE, FEELING FRAZZLED

Spotting your inner critic doesn't mean it packs up and leaves. It lingers like glitter after craft day—clinging to your routines, reactions, and relationships. Before long, life feels like a mental minefield, no matter how polished it looks on the outside. What it feeds on runs deeper: low self-worth. That's its power. And unless the root is healed, it will always find new disguises, whispering your deepest, darkest insecurities.

The critic loves the spotlight but rarely makes a grand entrance; it usually sneaks in through the back door and settles in before you even notice. Sometimes the result is a tear-streaked breakdown in a public restroom. Other times, it causes you to disguise yourself as who you think you should be. It looks like being overly "independent," saying yes when you mean no, or chasing perfection. And I was guilty of all of it. I thought if I were perfect, my critic couldn't complain. If I never showed emotion, no one could use my feelings against me. But here's the truth: that armor I wore? It wasn't strength; it was fear dressed up as productivity and approval-chasing. I honestly believed that if I performed flawlessly, I might finally like what I saw.

FLIP THE SCRIPT

One powerful tool you can use to disarm your inner critic is reframing. You've already seen how it began to change things in my story. Now, let's break it down so you can practice it yourself. It's not about sugarcoating reality; it's about replacing fear-based thoughts with something empowering.

Here's what that looks like:

- **Inner Critic:** *"Other people have it together. What's wrong with you?"*

- **Reframed:** *"I don't need to have it all together. I'm allowed to be a work in progress."*

It's a skill, and it takes practice. At first, it feels awkward. Like trying on confidence that doesn't quite fit...yet. But the more you stick with it, the easier it feels, until those new thoughts start sounding less like a script and more like *you.*

> *"Your inner critic is the voice of fear; stop listening."*

Tea Time with My Inner Critic

When I decided to go back to school for my master's, my inner critic showed up like an uninvited party guest—bullhorn in hand, zero chill, and absolutely no snacks. So, I had to put my new reframing tool to work immediately. The conversation went a little something like this:

Critic: *"What do you think you're doing?"*

Me: "Applying to grad school."

Critic: *"You don't even like school, and you're old."*

Me: "Plenty of people older than me graduate every day."

Critic: *"You'll fail, and everyone will judge you."*

Me: "No, I won't, but even if I fail, I'll learn."

Spoiler alert: I didn't finish the program. I completed five classes, got a 4.0 GPA... and then, for health reasons, I had to withdraw.

Cue the critic's victory lap!

At first, I felt embarrassed, like a total failure. I imagined people saying, "I knew she wasn't serious." But then I realized it didn't matter, because I finally had proof that my inner critic was wrong. I'd never earned a 4.0 before, and it wasn't luck. It was effort. It was evidence that my mind was capable, even when my body couldn't keep up. That realization brought a kind of peace I didn't expect.

For once, I wasn't at war with myself about it. I'd done my best, and that was enough. Sometimes peace doesn't come from pushing harder; it comes from knowing when to let go.

THE TRUTH HURTS, BUT IT ALSO HEALS

The inner critic loves the sound of its own voice. It drones on so long it can take the fight right out of you. Before I learned how to separate its voice from my own, I hid my pain behind a smile and pretended I was okay. I told everyone I was fine, but inside, I felt broken. With every exhausted step, my inner critic only got louder. I became more vulnerable to its lies until I realized they weren't just draining me, they were changing how I saw life and myself.

Then one day, I heard a speaker on YouTube ask, "How much do you love yourself?" My gut response was… *ehhh*, followed by *uh oh*. I didn't expect a random video to hit so hard, but it did. Then the speaker added, "You can't love anyone else until you love yourself."

That line stayed with me, mostly because my problem was the opposite. I've never struggled to love other people. I'm full of love, so why couldn't I keep even a little for myself? The truth was, my inner critic was draining it all. I had to learn to turn that love inward, which meant finally quieting the critic instead of letting it run the show.

WHEN YOUR INNER CRITIC IS DISGUISED AS "DRIVE"

As I started offering myself compassion, I also noticed how often I forgot it. Because when your default setting is get it done, softness doesn't come easily. But who has time for soft anyway? I was raised by a single mother, and strength ran in her veins. Soft wasn't an option, not for her, and definitely not for me.

Then I realized something else: I was tired. I hadn't just been hard on myself emotionally—I'd been performing strength like it was my job, and I'm pretty sure I was Employee of the Month. I prided myself on having the answers: the fixer, the doer, the one who had it handled. A full-on gladiator in leggings. (Olivia Pope would've been proud.)

I kept people at a distance so they wouldn't see me fracturing, piece by piece. From afar, I looked self-sufficient. But independence was my armor, and fear held the sword. What I didn't see back then was that version of me—the one who never asked for help, never showed weakness, and always kept it together—she wasn't real. She was a survival strategy, a funhouse reflection shaped by fear, pressure, and old expectations.

But survival isn't the same as being whole, and you can't build a peaceful life on a foundation of performance.

Perhaps you've been there too, always keeping it together and showing up even when you're running on fumes. That's the sneaky side of the inner critic: sometimes it doesn't shout insults; it just whispers, *keep going, don't stop, don't show weakness.*

So now, let's make it practical. We've talked about what the inner critic sounds like and how it wears you down. But the next step is learning to respond differently.

When that voice starts getting antsy, here are four small things you can try right now to shift the conversation.

1. Catch It & Call It Out

Ask yourself:

- Is this true?

2. Speak Back with Compassion

Your critic thrives on shame. Fight back with kindness.

Example:

- "I'm doing my best with what I have."

- "This is hard, and I'm allowed to struggle without tearing myself down."

- "Even if I mess up, I'm still worthy of love."

3. Create a "Truth Toolkit"

Write down 3–5 truths, mantras, or verses you can return to when you're spiraling.

Example toolkit:

- "Progress over perfection."

- "I am not behind; I'm on my own path."

(Stick it on your mirror, phone, laptop, wherever the critic tends to appear.)

4. Try the Younger Self Trick

When you're spiraling, pause and ask:

"What would I say to my younger self right?"

You deserve the same love and patience you'd give to little you, because they're still part of you. They're still learning, still healing, and still worthy of kindness, compassion, and the space to grow.

THE CRITIC HAD ITS SAY, NOW IT'S YOUR TURN

Just because your inner critic is loud doesn't mean it's right. Just because you're still working through things doesn't mean you're failing. Just because you haven't mastered self-love doesn't mean you're not worthy of it. You are still growing, and that, my friend, is more than enough.

After uncovering the voice running the show, it's time to take the mic back. But here's the thing: changing the narrative isn't just about affirmations and pep talks—though those help. It's about getting honest about what's underneath the noise. Sometimes, it's not just the critic that's hurting you; it's the things you tucked away because they felt too heavy, too raw, too much.

But what if the healing you've been waiting for is on the other side of that?

Up next: It's not the critic that has the final word. It's the pain you've been avoiding. And in the next chapter, we're going there.

Chapter 3

HEALING WHAT YOU'VE BEEN AVOIDING

We start picking up messages about who we are from parents, caregivers, teachers, and peers almost as soon as we can walk. Those messages start stacking up, building the foundation for how we see ourselves, for better, worse, or just plain confusing.

We may develop a strong sense of self if nurtured, encouraged, and treated with kindness. On the other hand, if what we faced was criticism, neglect, trauma, or love that felt conditional, we may have internalized the belief that something was wrong with us.

Trauma *can* appear with a Hollywood-level explosion, but more often, it's a series of tiny cuts—bullying at school, emotionally unavailable parents, unhealthy relationships, harsh criticism. Each one small, but together, they leave deep scars. Add societal pressure on top of that, and suddenly it feels like we're all losing an invisible competition we never even signed up for.

Little by little, your view of yourself shifts, fueling the warped reflection you've come to believe.

The good news? You can start seeing things clearly once you spot what's been distorting the picture. Your past may have gotten a few chapters, but it doesn't get to write the whole book. When you uncover the false beliefs beneath the surface, you can finally untangle them and start seeing yourself through truth, not through trauma.

For me, that realization was like flipping on a light. I saw the shadows for what they were and knew it was time to reclaim the driver's seat. But knowing where the distortion started wasn't enough; I had to face it head-on.

Healing doesn't come from pretending the past didn't happen. Still, many people (myself included) try to bury the hard stuff, hoping it'll disappear. But, surprise: it doesn't.

Ignored pain doesn't vanish; it reshapes itself and shows up in your life as:

• **Self-sabotage:** You mess up good things because you don't believe you deserve them.

• **Emotional numbness:** You shut down, not because you don't feel, but because feeling *anything* is too much.

• **Destructive cycles:** You keep attracting people who confirm your deepest insecurities about yourself.

To start rewriting your story, you have to acknowledge what happened and understand how it shaped you. When you face your past wounds, you take your power back. You stop letting the old stories define your worth. There's no need to pretend it didn't hurt you; what matters is that it doesn't get the last word.

> *"Avoidance feels safe until it starts costing you peace."*

THE HEALING STARTER PACK

Healing isn't a straight line. The question is, where do you begin when you're finally ready to face what you've been avoiding? I wish I could hand you a neat little checklist that fixed everything in a few quick steps. But healing doesn't work like that. It's messy, and sometimes it looks like two steps forward with one ugly cry back. Still, there are a few gentle places to start:

1. Seek Therapy & Professional Support

Talking to a therapist can change your life. Seriously. A good one will help you unpack old wounds, challenge negative thought patterns, and build a healthier version of you with no judgment, shame, or side-eyes. Therapy is not weakness; it's wisdom.

2. Journal for Reflection

Writing can be therapy, too. It's like unraveling all the noise in your head to hear your heart speak.

Try journaling about:

- A painful experience and how it reshaped you.

- A belief you have about yourself that might not be true.

- A time you overcame something difficult, and what it taught you.

3. Practice Mindfulness & Emotional Awareness

Mindfulness isn't about having a Zen Garden and meditating for hours. It means paying attention to what you feel and letting yourself *feel it,* without judgment. Instead of stuffing your emotions down with snacks and Netflix, try sitting with them. Notice them. Name them. Ask what they're trying to tell you. You're not required to act on every feeling, but ignoring them doesn't help either. Sometimes you need to let them pull up a chair, say their piece, and then move on.

4. Reframe Your Narrative

You are not what happened to you. You are who you've become despite it. So instead of saying something like "This broke me," try:

- What did I learn from this?

- How did it shape me for the better?

- Who did I become because I survived it?

You're not a victim of your story; you're the author. So, pick up the pen.

5. Cultivate Self-Compassion & Forgiveness

Forgiveness doesn't mean pretending it didn't hurt or excusing what happened. It means releasing the grip that pain has on your future. And that includes forgiving yourself, too. The inner critic may try to shame you, but you're doing your best with what you've got. So remind yourself: you are worthy of healing, you deserve love and respect, and you are not your past.

GYM-TIMIDATION, MIRROR AVOIDANCE, AND THE MOMENT EVERYTHING SHIFTED

Let's talk about what I avoided for years: taking care of my health. Truth be told, I was afraid. Scared that even if I tried, I'd fail. That I'd waste time, waste money, and still end up miserable in my own body. So, I told myself it wasn't that important. I shrugged off the comments, avoided mirrors, and stopped taking pictures. I didn't want to face the version of me that was shaped by fear and avoidance. The funhouse version felt easier to avoid than to confront.

Even when I wasn't overweight, I thought I was. And then, when I actually *was* overweight, I buried my head in the sand. People suggested gyms, diets, and trainers, and I had a whole playlist of excuses on loop:

- "I hate the gym."

- "I don't know how to use the equipment."

- "I'm too busy."

- "It's too expensive."

- "Tacos."

Then one day, I took a picture, and when I saw it, I hardly recognized the person staring back. It wasn't about looks but how far I'd wandered from myself. That was my enough-is-enough moment. I stopped chasing picture-perfect and got real. I wasn't trying to be swimsuit-ready (especially because I can't even swim). I just wanted to feel strong and be healthy. So, I hired a trainer and hated every minute, but I didn't quit. That's when I realized healing is learning to respect who you already are while growing stronger, little by little.

HALF GRIT, HALF GRACE

I wish healing were simple: work hard, stay disciplined, sweat it out. Easy, right? Except it wasn't. Healing asked for more than grit. It showed up when I learned the rhythm of effort and surrender—pushing forward while also letting go. It meant doing the work and trusting what I couldn't control.

Sometimes healing looked like showing up for therapy when I wanted to cancel, journaling through painful memories instead of ignoring them, setting boundaries even when guilt crept in, and trying again when I slipped back into old habits. Other times, it looked like surrender—letting go of control, trusting that I didn't have to fix everything perfectly, believing that God still had a plan for me even when I couldn't see it. It meant permitting myself to rest, to grieve, to feel, and realizing that God never asked me to carry it all alone.

One of my favorite reminders is this: "But he said to me, 'My grace is sufficient for you, for my power is made perfect in weakness.'" (2 Corinthians 12:9 NIV) That's the beauty of surrender—you're allowed to stumble, fall, and take the scenic route.

Work in Progress, Party of One

I'm writing this book, but that doesn't mean I have it all figured out. My big issue? The need for approval. I can be strong, self-aware, even confident, but I still secretly want someone to pat me on the shoulder and say, "Good job, you're doing great!" (Which is fine... until I start doubting myself when no one is around).

That craving for approval has been a lifelong companion. It kept me from facing the truth for a long time: I was avoiding my own voice. I wanted everyone else to clap for me because I didn't know how to clap for myself. And maybe, deep down, I needed their voices because mine alone wasn't loud enough to drown out my critic.

I'm still learning to quiet that need because the truth is, validation doesn't come from outside; it has to start within. Sometimes that means moving in silence, not explaining yourself, and finding peace in it.

Making your voice loud enough starts with learning to trust it and speaking to yourself with the same compassion and honesty you'd give a friend. The more you practice that, the less you need outside noise to remind you who you are.

Growth doesn't always feel like a breakthrough. Most of the time, it's giving yourself grace when you're not "healed enough" and reminding yourself that you don't have to be. Healing isn't a deadline; it's a journey.

FINAL THOUGHT

The first step in healing isn't about having all the answers; it's about asking better questions, like: "Whose story have I been living, and why am I still clinging to it?"

I want you to remember that you can show up exactly as you are. You're worthy of rest, love, and clarity without earning them. You don't have to shrink to fit spaces never meant for you. You were made to heal. You were made to become. And the moment you let go of what was never yours to carry, you create room to step into who you were truly meant to be.

Up next: Letting go is only the beginning. Next, we'll tackle what it means to see yourself clearly and why that changes everything.

Part 2

DEFINING YOUR PURPOSE &
REBUILDING YOUR CONFIDENCE

"You won't find your path by waiting; you find it by walking."

———◄◆O◆►———

This is where you stop shrinking and start stretching. Where you get clear on who you are, what you want, and why you deserve it. So let's start building the kind of life that actually fits you, from the inside out.

Chapter 4

SEEING YOURSELF CLEARLY

Let's talk about vision—not the 20/20 kind, but the kind that helps you stop walking through life on autopilot, exhausted and directionless. When you can't see clearly, the funhouse becomes your default, and you stop trusting your eyes. Having vision means you stop drifting and start steering. That doesn't mean everything goes perfectly; the world will still throw curveballs.

Still, you don't get tossed around as easily when you're anchored to your goals, values, and purpose. . You start moving with intention, building something real, and suddenly life feels like it actually belongs to *you*. I've heard so many motivational speakers talk about "knowing your why," but honestly, I didn't get it at first. I grew up hearing about "goals" and "dreams," not "vision" and "why."

What I've come to realize is that each one plays a different role, but together, they shape the bigger picture. It's the difference between reacting to life and actually living it on purpose—vision gives you direction, goals are the steps, and your why is the foundation.

And then there's clarity—vision's long-lost cousin who shows
up late but always brings perspective. They work together when
you're pursuing your goals, but each plays a different role. *Clarity*
reveals your starting point; it helps you see where you are, what
you want, and how to move forward confidently. It sharpens your
options, highlights your strengths, and cuts through the mental
fog so you can make better decisions. *Vision*, on the other hand,
is the bigger picture, the future you're working toward, and the
kind of life you want to build. Clarity keeps you grounded in the
present; vision keeps you motivated for the long haul. You need
both: clear insight helps you choose your next step, and vision
reminds you why you're taking it.

Here's where it gets personal. Want a big house? Cool—why? Is
it to show off, or because you want your family to have enough
space to gather? Want to make $200K a year? Great—but is it
for designer bags, to retire your spouse, or to travel while your
knees still work? There are no right or wrong answers. It's about
knowing what's true for you. That's the kind of clarity that brings
purpose and steadies you when fear tries to knock you off course.

SEARCHING FOR A SIGN (AND STILL PAYING BILLS)

I've spent most of my time floating through life, with no clear path
and no idea where I'd land. I once heard a girl on TV say she felt
like she was born at the wrong time and didn't quite fit in this
world. And I thought, *yup, Haley gets me.* My biggest pain point?
I couldn't figure out my reason for existing. If I was created on
purpose, for a purpose, why couldn't I figure out what it was?

Everyone around me seemed to have it all figured out pretty
quickly. Meanwhile, I took every personality test known to
man—some out of curiosity, but most out of desperation. I
met with college career counselors, hired more as an adult, and
read enough self-help books to qualify for an honorary PhD.

Apparently, I'm an ISFJ that's "conventional and enterprising." But did any of that hand me a life blueprint? Nope.

To be clear, I'm not saying career or personality assessments are useless. The Myers-Briggs test (aka 16 Personalities) actually gave me something I'd been missing: insight. It helped me understand why I was so miserable in so many of my jobs, they went against everything that made me... well, me. Reading my results felt like someone had been following me around with a clipboard—every strength, every struggle, perfectly noted.

What surprised me most was how much I changed over time. In college, I was an ISTJ—very black-and-white, logic-first, feelings-last. These days, I still think logically (and can be blunt more often than not), but I've learned to leave room for the gray areas. To actually consider emotions. To let things be flawed and layered.

And honestly? That shift says a lot. There's something really cool about being able to see your growth in black and white—to watch the letters shift as your heart softens and your mind opens. Seeing my personality breakdown felt like finding a map—not one that led to a perfect destination, but one that helped me say, "Not that. That's not for me."

And yet, with all that insight, I still had no idea what color my parachute was. (I did figure out my love language, though, so... small wins.) I still needed to figure out why I was put on this earth and how to pay my bills while I sorted it out. So I kept working jobs I hated, because let's be honest, the electric company doesn't care about my identity crisis. I stayed stuck in my damaged reality, convinced I wasn't capable, ready, or clear enough to do something different.

The only thing I knew for sure was this: I wanted more than survival. I wanted to live.

NO DREAM JOB, JUST A DREAM LIFE

My therapist once asked me to picture my dream life. What would it look like? What would it feel like? What wouldn't it include? Thanks to the little "map" those personality tests handed me, it became surprisingly easy to name what I didn't want: stress disguised as success, environments that valued performance over peace, roles that drained me instead of helping me grow.

That's when it clicked: clarity doesn't always come from knowing exactly what you want. Sometimes it comes from knowing what you're done tolerating. That changed everything. I stopped obsessing over job titles or five-year plans and started asking myself what kind of life I actually wanted to wake up to.

In my mind, I began to see it: the mornings, the spaces, the work that felt purposeful instead of just profitable. I pictured slow starts with sunlight spilling through the blinds, coffee in hand, peace instead of panic. I imagined warm spaces filled with little reminders of what matters most.

I pictured how I wanted to feel when no one was watching: steady, content, unhurried. I wondered what peace might look like in the small, in-between moments, and how freedom and love could weave their way into my ordinary days until they became my new normal.

No, I didn't suddenly discover my one true calling or a color-coded plan for the next decade. Still, I had something better: hope. And that was enough to take one step, then another, until the pieces of who I wanted to be started to take shape.

> *"You don't need all the answers to move, just enough light to take the next step."*

CLARITY THROUGH THERAPY (AND A LITTLE FAITH)

One of the best decisions I ever made was going to therapy. I needed answers, but what I really needed was someone to help me see myself clearly. I know some people are skeptical about therapy, thinking things like:

- *I should be able to figure this out on my own.*

- *What if they judge me?*

- *They can't fix my problems.*

- *What if it doesn't work?*

Truthfully? I get it. Some of those feelings are valid. It *is* weird to bare your soul—and your mistakes—to a stranger. Especially knowing that they can't "fix you," but they can help you fix yourself.

My experience has been very positive. I've had two very different therapists, and both gave me the perspective I desperately needed. Not every therapist will be the right fit, and even when they are, growth is still uncomfortable. But if you're open to it, therapy can unlock a whole new level of understanding about where you've been and where you want to go.

Enter: faith. I didn't grow up in church, but never questioned whether God was real. While therapy helped me unpack the "what" and the "how," faith gave me another piece: the quiet certainty that I wasn't here by accident. That even when I couldn't see the complete picture, God could. The more I studied the Bible, the more I saw it everywhere—a gentle reassurance that purpose isn't something you force your way into; it unfolds, one step at a time.

Therapy helped me untangle the mess, and faith gave me permission to keep moving, even when the road ahead still felt foggy. But before I could see my future clearly, I had to make peace with the girl I used to be.

DELETE. RENAME. RECLAIM

Growing up, I always felt a little lost in the shuffle. My brothers were older, already building their own lives while I was still trying to figure out who I was.

I looked up to them, and their approval carried almost as much weight as my mom's. They're also ridiculously talented, which only added to the pressure. There's a fine line between admiring someone and wishing you had what they did, and I've been toeing that line my whole life. I just wanted to believe there was something that made me special, too.

I wasn't a star athlete, super smart, or tech-savvy. Me? I'm... sarcastic—a talent that doesn't exactly shine, except when someone needs a perfectly timed one-liner. I'm also the baby of the family and the only girl. Honestly, I figured the only things that made me special were my spot in the lineup and my gender. I felt like a blank canvas someone forgot to paint, or a shadow in the corner of the room—present, but never defined.

Back then, I would've taken any label: "the pretty one," " the brave one ," "the creative one." Because a label meant someone saw something in me worth naming, I now see it differently. That blankness was its own strange little gift. It gave me freedom and responsibility. No one had decided my identity, which meant I had to figure it out for myself. I was free to choose. To create. To write my own story.

As I got older, I realized something else: some labels don't just describe you, they confine you. Some were handed names they never asked for, like "the troublemaker," "the drama queen," "the difficult child," "the needy one." After a while, people start conforming to those definitions, even if they don't quite fit. That's where the damage begins. It's like looking into someone else's mirror and being told, "This is who you are," even when everything inside you knows it's not. Healing means taking your identity back instead of accepting the one others assigned you.

Update: I'm still not as talented as they are. People don't call me when something breaks or to whip up a perfect meal. But they do call when they're overwhelmed or hurting. When they need to vent or untangle something too heavy to carry alone. That's my gift. My talent. My thing. And I'm so thankful I gave myself the space to grow into it.

DEAR ME, BUCKLE UP

One of the most surprising things my therapist asked me to do was write a letter to my younger self. I groaned, stalled, and thought, *This is so cheesy.* I almost skipped the exercise altogether, but it unlocked parts of my story I hadn't touched in years. It gave me space to connect the dots between where I've been, where I got stuck, and where I want to go.

So here it is, a piece of me, in case it speaks to a piece of you.

Dearest Me,

First of all, breathe. I know you've carried way too much for way too long. You've asked yourself if something was wrong with you, if maybe God skipped your name when He was handing out purpose. You smiled through heartbreak, pushed through doubt, sat on the sidelines, and questioned everything like your worth, your voice...basically, your whole existence. But you kept going.

I'm giving you grace for being too hard on yourself. For trusting the wrong people. For believing you had to earn love, peace, even rest.

And I'm also thanking you for surviving. For staying kind. For not giving up when the way forward felt like a maze.

You didn't miss your purpose. You were moving toward it the whole time, even when it felt like you were standing still. Confusion isn't failure. You're not behind. You've just been busy surviving.

I want you to know that it gets better. We are still growing, but we're finally able to love who we are. And that's because of you.

Sincerely,

Me. You. Us.

A Letter Only You Can Write

Want clarity? Talk to the version of you who didn't have any. Ask what they feared, what they needed, and what they dreamed of but never said out loud. Then write them a letter that's kind, honest, and real. Don't worry about "writing it right"; this is about honesty, not grammar. And if you need help getting started, here are some prompts to guide you:

1. Acknowledge the Pain You Felt

- "I know you were hurting, even when you didn't show it."

- "You were holding so much inside, and I wish someone had noticed how heavy it was."

2. Recognize Your Effort and Strength

- "You kept going even when it felt pointless, which took courage."

- "You were so much stronger than you gave yourself credit for."

3. Show Compassion for Mistakes or Regrets

- "You did the best you could with what you knew then."

- "I forgive you for being hard on yourself. You deserved more kindness, especially from yourself."

4. Validate Your Dreams and Fears

- "Your dreams weren't silly. They mattered then, and still do now."

- "I know you were scared. You didn't know what was ahead, but kept showing up anyway."

5. Offer Gratitude and Love

- "Thank you for not giving up."

- "I love who you were, even if you couldn't see your worth."

6. Reframe Painful Memories with Grace

- "That heartbreak didn't destroy you; it revealed your capacity to feel deeply."

- "That failure wasn't the end; it was the start of turning into someone wiser."

7. End with Hope

- "You're not stuck in that chapter anymore. We made it out."

- "You may not have seen it then, but something beautiful was growing inside you."

No Map? No Problem. Start Walking

You can't really know where you're going until you've been honest about where you've been. That's why exercises that make you pause, like writing to your past self or simply reflecting, matter. If you don't know your history, you're likely to repeat it. And you'll never find your way if you're clinging to the past.

Sure, some people stumble into purpose by accident, but most of us grow into it step by step, choice by choice. You begin to recognize it when you start understanding who you really are, because you can't find your way until you've found yourself.

But the path doesn't wait for you to feel ready; it starts unfolding the moment you take one deliberate step. It's about being honest with yourself, your story, and what you want. That's when things begin to change. You realize confidence isn't always natural; for many of us, it's practiced, not gifted. You see that you don't need a ten-step plan; you just need a starting point, like honesty, hope, or one small step toward the life you actually want.

Up next: If self-doubt is the shadow, confidence is the light. In the next chapter, we'll explore the truth about confidence and how to grow it in real life.

Chapter 5

THE TRUTH ABOUT CONFIDENCE (IT'S NOT WHAT YOU THINK)

I used to think of myself as a puzzle, and not a single piece resembled confidence. I doubted my voice, my talent, my drive to succeed. And I placed far too much importance on my appearance, as if my reflection could prove my worth. Dress it up on the outside, and the inside would somehow catch up or so I thought. But that kind of confidence was surface-level, held together with lip gloss and anxiety. And I suspect I'm not the only one.

Many of us were taught that confidence and appearance go hand in hand: throw on the right outfit, and poof...confidence appears. *Fake it till you make it,* right? Except that's not the whole story. Confidence isn't about looking perfect, dressing flawlessly, or being the prettiest in the room. I just wish I had gotten that memo sooner.

My signature look? Clear mascara and cozy vibes, quite the opposite of "bombshell." So, of course, I assumed I needed to step it up. After all, I grew up hearing *"men are visual."* Translation: give them something worth looking at.

Then one day, I was peacefully relaxing and watching *Awkward* when this line assaulted me with extreme prejudice: "When you're pretty, you're happy. And clearly, you're not happy."

Warped, I know, but that's when I realized: *I am Jenna.*

Yes, I know it's fiction, but hear me out. Jenna was a girl who didn't fit society's version of beauty—longing to feel comfortable in her own skin and accepted as she was—yet made to believe it would never happen unless she changed. So you see...she is me, and I am her.

One minute, I was casually binging a show; the next, I was under attack in my own home. It felt less like a teenage dramedy and more like someone had slipped me a "Carefrontation Letter" through the TV screen—signed, sealed, and delivered by my inner critic. Peaceful day... over.

Truthfully, the freedom to be myself *should* have made me happy; after all, isn't that what we all want? To breathe, to relax, to stop chasing approval? But I had a warped perspective. Happiness is an inside job, yet I was measuring mine with the wrong yardstick. By simply being myself, I assumed I wasn't trying hard enough. I wasn't *pretty enough, polished enough, anything enough.*

I could be myself around the people I loved; they were my safe space. But in relationships, I twisted into a version I thought would earn love, losing pieces of myself in the process. Years slipped by like that: me pretending, them undeserving. The result? A whole lot of anxiety and even more self-doubt. I wasn't being authentic, and deep down, I knew it.

That's the Funhouse Mirror for you. It distorts enough to sell you the lie: *If you bend far enough, you'll finally feel worthy.* But bending to fit in is not the same as belonging.

REDEFINING BEAUTY, REDEFINING CONFIDENCE

As the years unfolded, I found myself drawn to women who, like me, didn't fit society's mold and didn't care to. Some didn't wear makeup, own designer clothes, or fit into a perfect size six. And yet... they radiated *real*.

I already knew confidence was more than appearance by this point, but I still struggled to shake the old programming. Watching these women laugh freely and live boldly began to reshape how I saw beauty. It wasn't about being flawless; it was about being authentic.

I knew I would never be confident if I couldn't shake the deep belief that I was less than and learn to stand in my truth. So I started with my appearance, since you can't solve the whole puzzle at once. And the truth I found was simple: I wanted to wear ponytails, comfy clothes, and tennis shoes—and still feel worthy of love and acceptance. In choosing to be unapologetically myself, I hope to give other women the strength to do the same.

That's what these amazing women did for me. They're imperfect, but more importantly, they're thoughtful, honest, and at ease in their own skin. That's the kind of confidence I'm working toward—not because they've mastered everything or have it all together, but because they keep showing up as themselves. And that kind of self-trust? It grows with every honest step you take.

So if you've ever wondered whether your quirks, scars, or differences make you "less than," let me say this clearly: they don't. Being different isn't a flaw. It's your superpower.

CONFIDENCE OR GOOD ACTING?

Accepting my differences was step one, but living confidently in them was a journey all its own. It's one thing to stop apologizing for who you are; it's another to believe you can stand tall in it. Just because you want to change doesn't mean it's automatic; sometimes the mask feels more comfortable. And if you haven't learned the difference between perceived and authentic confidence, you may struggle to take it off.

Perceived confidence is all about image: smiling big, looking put together, while your soul quietly sends SOS messages to the universe. Authentic confidence is different because it's not curated for show. It's rooted in healing, self-respect, and trust in who you are...even when no one's clapping. It's the kind that stays steady and reminds you that even if you fail, you still matter.

Plenty of people go for years, sometimes decades, projecting confidence that doesn't match how they feel. The tricky part? You can get so used to wearing the mask that you forget it's there. But you can't build authentic confidence if you're always performing.

For my acting debut, I was cast as the "Strong Friend"—the one people came to when they needed a soft place to land, but who never let anyone see her fall apart. I nailed the role but hated the script. Being there for others wasn't the problem; pretending I didn't need the same support was. I had people who cared, but I wouldn't let them in—not really. And it cost me connection. I was lonely, not because I wasn't loved, but because I wasn't confident enough to let anyone see me struggle.

If you're wondering whether you've been living with perceived confidence, here are some "looking confident, but not feeling it" moments you might recognize:

- **Job Interview:** Smiling through uncertainty, trying to believe I belong here.

- **Public Speaking:** Projecting confidence while battling chaos in your head.

- **Dressing Boldly:** Rocking the look while doubting the body underneath.

- **Social Events:** Looking social while secretly planning your escape.

- **Setting a Boundary:** Speaking up, then spiraling with guilt.

If any of this sounds familiar, exhale. You've carried a lot to make it here. But existing isn't the same as living. Now, you get to build something true, starting with one brave step. Because real confidence doesn't grow in darkness, it grows in being seen...mess and all.

CONFIDENCE COMES FROM DOING, NOT DAYDREAMING

By now, you've probably figured out I'm not exactly a risk-taker. We've already talked about how my return to school was a giant leap of faith. But let's rewind to an earlier confidence booster: high school—Afro-Haitian dance class. (Yes, that was a thing at my school. And yes, it was awesome.)

I loved it, but I played it safe in the intermediate class. So when senior year rolled around and the only class that fit my schedule was advanced, my heart sank. These kids were pros. To make things worse, a few girls already had it out for me because I was dating a popular football player. (Welcome back to Teen Drama 101.)

I wanted to forget it, but it was my last semester and my last chance to dance. Thankfully, my teacher encouraged me, and a friend agreed to sign up too. So I enrolled and kept showing up, mistakes and all. Eventually, I learned the dances, found my rhythm, and performed on stage like I always did at the end of the year.

The advanced class even danced at our high school graduation, in front of thousands of people (yes, thousands). That's a massive leap from the girl terrified to enroll just months earlier. The experience wasn't perfect; there were hiccups. But it was empowering. And if I hadn't tried, I would've regretted it.

> *"Confidence doesn't mean you're not scared. It means you do it scared, anyway."*

Took Me Four Decades, but Who's Counting?

Looking back, that dance class gave me my first real glimpse of how confidence *felt,* not just how it looked. But I was still years away from untangling the truth about confidence, self-worth, and why both matter.

My latest confidence boost doesn't take us back quite so far. The story goes something like this: *once upon a time, a girl turned forty and thought it might kill her...*

Dramatic? Maybe. But I was genuinely upset. I braced for impact like a meteor headed straight for my fragile ego. Why? Because ages twenty-nine to thirty-nine felt like a slow walk through failure. I didn't have the career, the husband, the kids, or the picket fence. How could I already be middle-aged when my life hadn't even begun?

My friends were busy checking off life goals like items on a
grocery list, while I was still trying to figure out if I even
wanted that Pleasantville life. Career...yes. Husband...yes. Picket
fence...maybe. Kids? No clue. Perhaps I did want them, or maybe I
just liked the idea of having a little broke best friend to share snacks
with.

To make matters worse, the generation after me started getting
married, having babies, and buying homes. I had changed their
diapers, and now I was attending their baby showers. It felt like
I was walking the plank. One wrong move and I'd slip into a sea
of despair. I didn't want balloons, I wanted answers. A memo. A
burning bush. *Something*—but then, plot twist, my 40th birthday
was amazing.

I was on a family camping trip when my niece threw me a party.
I was rocking a birthday sash and a tiara, celebrating with food,
music, games, cake, and more tequila shots than I care to admit.
(Still not sure how I remembered the night.) I laughed, sang, and
got teased about my "cougar" status and being born "way, *way*
back in the '80s." It should've made me feel old, but instead, I felt
amazing—and the weirdest part? I kept feeling amazing even after
I got home.

Something inside began to unravel. For once, the "shoulds" didn't
consume me. It felt like I'd finally ripped up my funhouse ticket
and returned to the light of day. I wasn't obsessed with everything I
didn't have. I was simply... me. And for once, that felt like enough.
My cousin once told me that being in your 40s is freeing because
you stop letting the "checklist" define your worth. Back then, I
didn't believe her. But now, I get it.

NOT MAGIC. JUST REPETITION

I spent years believing I'd missed the confidence window. But
I wasn't lacking confidence; I was lacking evidence. I didn't

think I was capable of much... because I hadn't tried much. Confidence doesn't arrive polished and ready; it appears in the mess—mid-panic, mid-progress, mid *what am I even doing?* It grows one step at a time. It took years and more than a few breakdowns to accept that.

I wish I could tell you there's some magical formula. But confidence doesn't strike out of nowhere and change everything. It comes from practice. It's built in small, repeatable habits—the tiny things you keep doing, even when you feel like you're failing.

Here are a few things that help me stay grounded, especially on days when I'm questioning everything:

1. The "Three Truths" Practice

Each morning (or night), say or write three truths about yourself:

- "I am doing the best I can."

- "I don't have to prove anything today."

- "I deserve love and rest."

2. Mirror Check-Ins

Look in the mirror and say something kind to yourself. It might feel awkward at first, but it changes how you talk to yourself over time.

3. Weekly "Proof List"

Write down small wins. Even tiny things. Like:

- "I got out of bed even when I didn't want to."

- "I asked for help."

- "I said no when I needed to."

4. Internal Gratitude

Instead of only being thankful for what's around you, focus inward:

- "I'm grateful for how I keep trying."

- "I'm proud of the way I stayed patient today."

- "I love that I didn't let fear make the decision.

5. Quick Confidence Boosters

Simple habits that pull you back to center:

- Reflect on Moments of Pride

- Ask for Positive Feedback

- Practice Daily Gratitude

- Start a Strengths Journal

WHEN YOU STILL DON'T FEEL CONFIDENT... AND SHOW UP ANYWAY

Do I still struggle with confidence? Absolutely. I always joke that I'm one of those women who can't do anything, but truth be told, it's not that I can't; I just don't want to mess anything up. The women in my family are total DIY queens, so I've definitely caught the inferiority bug. And even if they weren't endlessly handy, they also have husbands to handle whatever they can't.

Unfortunately, I don't have the luxury of writing out a "honey-do" list—because honey, there's no one to do it. So I had to start trying things, and much to my surprise, I wasn't a total disaster. Sure, I'm not Martha Stewart or Bob the Builder (I draw the line at power tools), but I realized I didn't need to be great; I just needed to be willing. I guess functional is the new fabulous.

THE QUESTION THAT CHANGES EVERYTHING

If confidence comes from action, and self-worth from identity... What happens when you stop performing and start trusting yourself? When you stop accepting the distorted version and believe the real one? When you stop waiting to be perfect and decide to show up as you are? Can you wear clear mascara, rock a tiara, and still be a force? *Absolutely.*

Up next: What if the biggest thing holding you back... is you? In the next chapter, we'll tackle self-sabotage head-on and learn how to move forward with clarity.

Chapter 6

STOP SELF-SABOTAGING AND START MOVING FORWARD

Self-sabotage isn't weakness. It isn't laziness. It isn't even a character flaw. It's a habit, a protective reflex that shows up and convinces you to stay small. It's like staying in the pool's shallow end: you feel safe where your feet touch the ground, but you'll never know the beauty of drifting weightless, where fear gives way to freedom and trust becomes second nature.

Sometimes, it disguises itself as productivity, with endless planning instead of doing. Other times, it hides behind perfectionism, or whispers through quiet doubts: *I'll mess it up. I'm not smart enough.* It compares, delays, overthinks, and pretends to protect you from failure when it's really protecting you from growth.

That's the quiet cruelty of it. It starts small—just hesitation—but before long, you're bracing for disappointment instead of reaching for possibility.

Joy? Sounds Risky

Sabotaging habits don't just show up in daily routines. They get even more creative when hearts are on the line. If you've ever stayed in an unhealthy relationship because at least it was something, or pushed away someone great because you knew they'd eventually leave anyway—yep, that's self-sabotage too—and I know it all too well. Let's take another stroll down memory lane...

Early in my twenties, there was a guy who genuinely cared for me. Sweet, supportive, emotionally available, the complete package. We'd been friends for years, and after my love life crashed and burned, I thought, *this is it! My chance to be loved right.*

So naturally... I ruined it.

To quote the great Eric Forman from *That '70s Show*: "I ruined it. And I knew I was ruining it... and I just kept on ruining it." That was me. I got distant and cryptic, eventually telling him I couldn't do it. The truth? I was scared to be vulnerable, trust again, or hope. And instead of giving him a chance or giving myself one, I let fear drive the whole thing into the ground.

Yes, I was young, but I still regret it. Two decades later, the sting has softened but never really left. Even so, I believe it was for the best. I wasn't ready for a relationship, and if we had continued, I probably would've hurt him in other ways. So I like to think I spared him the worst of it in the long run. Still, I could've been more honest, more respectful of his feelings. He deserved better. And our friendship never recovered.

Fast forward ten years, and I still let fear call the shots. I was semi-single, fully displeased, and mid-vent (as I often was). Afterward, my niece looked at me and said, "I think you're afraid of being happy." I laughed it off, pretending she was being dramatic while secretly nursing my hurt feelings because... rude. But the line? It stuck, like that song *Call Me Maybe.* And the more I thought about it, the more I realized she was right.

Admitting that was hard. Because if I was afraid of being happy, then it meant I wasn't just unlucky in love—I was getting in my own way. It meant I had to face the fact that joy felt dangerous to me, because the higher I climbed, the harder the fall would be. Coming to terms with that took time and more than a few tears.

I eventually realized why it was so hard for me to shake those feelings. Fear doesn't disappear with age; it grows alongside you. And happiness? That's high stakes. Once you have something good, the risk of losing it feels overwhelming. Add relationships to the mix, and the stakes skyrocket.

Love means handing someone your heart and trusting it not to shatter if they stomp on it. That's a lot of trust for someone without the best track record and fear knows it. So it waits quietly, only speaking up when I'm ready to try again: *Be careful,* it whispers. Then, with a raised eyebrow and a smirk: *You sure you wanna get your hopes up?*

So I stall, hesitate, and ghost joy—just in case it plans to ghost me first. Not because it's wrong, but because it feels a little too right. And fear loves to ruin a good thing before it even begins.

But it was in that tension that faith started to meet me. I realized that if I was ever going to live fully, love deeply, and hope freely, I had to believe one thing: Even if I lost something, I wouldn't lose myself.

THE STOMACH AND THE TREADMILL

Of course, knowing that truth in my head didn't stop fear from sneaking in through other doors. And the easiest target was my body. I'd faced that battle before, and I really did want to get healthy at first. But my focus shifted somewhere between the scrolling, the comments, and the comparisons. It wasn't about health anymore. It became about being wanted—preferably with abs.

Not all self-sabotage looks like chaos. Sometimes it looks like control, like trying to fix yourself just enough to finally feel worthy. I thought that if I could control one thing—my weight—everything else would fall into place as if my Funhouse Mirror would suddenly burst into flames and reveal the real me underneath.

Which brings me to Exhibit A: my stomach. I was convinced that if it were flat, I'd finally feel whole—confident, beautiful, sexy. My disdain for my stomach started in high school, because my boyfriend was constantly picking at me. He did rude things like buying us matching couple shirts, but he bought mine a size too small. Then he told me we'd take pictures when I could fit it. (Needless to say, that picture never happened.)

In time, I realized that fixing the outside would never heal what was broken inside. I asked myself: what would actually make me happy? Wearing a crop top... or vegging out on the couch with pizza and snacks? After careful consideration, I decided: I'm a foodie through and through. Sweet or salty, pancakes, or pasta, if it's delicious, I'm interested.

And honestly, I'm always cold. A crop top doesn't suit me anyway. Give me leggings and oversized sweaters any day. Comfort is my love language, and if it comes in soft cotton or fleece, even better.

For those who don't have a food obsession to gain insight, here's something else to consider: **the hedonic treadmill.** It's a psychological concept that basically says this: we think we know what will make us happy, like a flat stomach, a new car, the dream house, but as soon as we get it, we adapt. Almost instantly, the high fades, and we start chasing the next thing. It's a never-ending cycle.

So losing my tummy wouldn't have fixed anything, at least not for long. Genuine joy lives in purpose, connection, gratitude, growth, and being true to yourself—even when your stomach isn't photo-ready.

Eventually, I did lose weight, but for the right reasons. I still have a little tummy, though. The difference is, I don't hate myself for it anymore. Self-loathing and peace don't mix, so I chose peace. And that matters more than the photo, the shirt, or the boy ever did.

> *"You can't build peace on fear or grow love from shame. The soil has to change before the garden can bloom."*

YOU CAN'T PRAY AWAY WHAT YOU KEEP PROTECTING

Growth isn't just about self-acceptance; you must stop hiding behind the walls you've built for protection. You can't ask for healing while holding onto the things still hurting you. My biggest wall is dating. I've prayed for peace, but I still spiral. One minute I'm convinced no man is worth the risk, the next I'm shouting, *"Okay, universe, I'm ready for love!"* Then, before the night's over, I'm trauma bonding with my girls and blasting the men-ain't-ish playlist like gospel. Mixed messages? Just a smidge.

I've talked about surrender before, but it's been harder in this area because of some awful experiences. For me, living by faith means telling God, "I'm scared, but I trust You more than I trust my past." It looks like opening my heart to hope, going on dates without scripting the breakup, and stopping myself from labeling every man a walking red flag.

Deep down, I want to believe what God says about love and partnership:

→ That "he who finds a wife finds what is good and receives favor from the Lord" (Proverbs 18:22 NIV).

→ That "two are better than one... if either of them falls down, one can help the other up" (Ecclesiastes 4:9–10 NIV).

→ That the right person won't just take from me, but sharpen me "as iron sharpens iron" (Proverbs 27:17 NIV).

And someday, I want to be able to say without hesitation or fear:

→ "I have found the one whom my soul loves." (Song of Solomon 3:4 NIV).

It takes faith to believe in love again and grace to admit that what I thought was love... wasn't. So I'm showing up with a surrendered heart and a willingness to participate in my healing. That means pausing when old habits resurface, breathing instead of bolting, and staying when my heart says flee. To trust that real love won't cost me my peace, but will reflect the One who created it. I choose not to run—not from hope, not from healing, and not from the kind of love I still believe is possible.

TRYING TO BLOOM WITH ROOTS IN CEMENT

Even when your hands are open and your heart is ready, you can still miss what God is giving if your soul is anchored in unworthiness. Healing depends on where you plant your faith. Damaged roots can't nurture growth; even miracles can feel like mistakes when your soul is crowded with doubt.

Maybe you want something more—peace, love, success, or just a break from the noise—but the problem isn't the goal. It's the story underneath, whispering that you'll never have it. If that belief stays buried, no effort will ever feel like enough. You'll stay stuck, running in circles and wondering why nothing ever changes.

I still wrestle with that old voice: *You're not good enough. You'll mess it up. No one will stay.* Some days it's muted; other days it's in surround sound. But I keep showing up anyway. That's the work. Healing doesn't mean silencing those thoughts forever; it means learning to respond differently when they appear.

If you're ready to start breaking the cycle, take it slow and trust that small steps still count. Notice when self-doubt tries to pull you under, and pause long enough to ask yourself: *Is this helping me grow or holding me back?* Then focus on micro-moves instead of massive leaps.

Sabotage thrives on all-or-nothing thinking, but small steps taken with intention can shift everything. Maybe that looks like sending the email, going for a walk, setting the boundary, or writing the page. Whatever it is, just move.

FINAL THOUGHTS

Self-sabotage isn't about a lack of discipline. It's about fear, trauma, misalignment, and the exhaustion that comes from constantly trying to protect yourself. But what if the thing you're scared to lose was never yours to carry, just another warped reflection you've already outgrown? What if peace doesn't come from controlling everything, but from learning to rest, receive, and believe you're safe without the armor?

So here's your permission slip: let go. Try. Take the next step. And when you do, protect that progress.

Up next: setting boundaries confidently, even when you've been afraid to say no.

Part 3

WALKING IN CONFIDENCE & TAKING ACTION

"Healing is only the beginning, now it's time to live like you believe it."

———————◆O◆———————

This is where everything shifts from insight to impact. You've done the inner work; now comes the outer transformation. It's time to set boundaries without guilt, rest without shame, and surround yourself with people who see your worth even when you forget. No more shrinking, no more self-silencing. This is your permission to take up space, walk in purpose, and live boldly in your truth.

Chapter 7

SETTING BOUNDARIES WITHOUT GUILT

Working on self-worth? Awesome! But don't forget self-respect. They may walk side by side, but they're not the same. Self-worth asks, *Do you like who you are?* Self-respect asks, *Do you treat yourself like you matter?* And the thread that ties them together? Boundaries.

They're more than rules; they're proof. They show you believe you're worthy of respect and deserving of care. They set the standard for how others treat you *and* how you treat yourself. And here's the best part: every time you honor a boundary, you strengthen your self-worth, reinforce your self-respect, and raise the bar for how you expect to be treated.

They help you protect your energy, avoid burnout, and prioritize your peace. Because when you set clear limits and honor them, you're not only saying no. You're saying yes to the version of you who knows better. You're saying, *I matter. My needs matter.*

And the more you practice, the easier it gets to spot that old funhouse image whispering: *Soften. Settle. Stay quiet*...Not today, distortion. Not today.

Bottom line? You can't build real self-worth without learning how to protect it. Troy had walls for a reason, but they let something in that looked harmless, and it destroyed them from the inside out. That's what happens when you let guilt, fear, or people-pleasing slip past your boundaries. So remember: No Trojan horses allowed.

MAKING ROOM FOR YOU

If you hate disappointing people, dread confrontation, or feel guilty for putting yourself first, boundaries will probably feel uncomfortable for a while. For some, it's hard because they don't know where their limits begin or end. Many of us didn't grow up seeing boundaries modeled in healthy ways, so trying to set them now can feel awkward or even wrong, like we're breaking some unspoken contract we never actually signed. And if you've spent years managing everyone else's comfort, your needs can start to feel negotiable.

But boundaries aren't about pushing people away; they're about making space for what you actually need. That's not selfish; it's survival. And while knowing that is one thing, doing it is another, especially when you care about people who need limits.

Boundaries are essential because they allow you to breathe, heal, and live without burning yourself out. They help you prioritize your needs, protect your energy, and remind you that you matter. When you honor your limits, you reduce stress, prevent burnout, and treat yourself with the same respect you offer others. Boundaries also give you the freedom to make choices that align with your values instead of everyone else's expectations. And the best part? They don't distance you from others; they deepen the connection by building trust, honesty, and mutual respect.

Boundaries aren't barriers; they're doors. Every time you set one, you're not shutting people out; you're letting the healthiest version of yourself step in.

> *"Saying 'no' doesn't make you mean. It makes you mindful."*

TOO BOOKED FOR GUILT TRIPS

A while back, I planned a trip, and a close friend really wanted to come. I love this person, but I knew their energy would throw off the entire vibe, and the last thing I wanted was to spend my vacation managing someone else's needs. I wanted to relax. Did I tell them that? Of course not. Instead, I made excuses that it was too last-minute and everything was already booked. Technically true, but mostly? I just didn't want them to come.

Why was honesty so hard? Because my heart was involved. When it's someone you love, self-protection can get blurry. I didn't want to hurt their feelings. And if I'm being sincere, maybe I couldn't speak up because I believed their feelings mattered more than mine.

What would I say now? "I've been craving this trip because I need peace, space, and freedom. I care about you, but I can't ignore what I need.

Learning to say no without guilt is difficult for most of us, but it's one of the most freeing things you can do. Each "no" is an act of self-respect, creating room for the "yes" that supports your peace and priorities.

BOUNDARIES AND BESTIES: A SURVIVAL STORY

Since I'm telling stories about friends, we must discuss my BFF. We're complete opposites, think spotlight and shadow, extrovert energy and introvert peace. She thrives on constant connection. I need regular alone time, or I'll snap. We've known each other since middle school and are now more family than friends. But our journey hasn't been without bumps

Case in point: it took years for her to accept that when I say, "I need time to myself," it's not personal, it's preservation. When I tried to explain this to her as a kid, she was so offended, you'd think I kicked her dog or something. But I stood my ground, and she came to understand. Now, when I say the magic words *"me time,"* she rolls her eyes, laughs, and says, "okay." I know that boundary saved our friendship, and it taught me that if someone truly loves you, they'll respect your needs even if they don't always understand them.

That's how it should be; setting limits shouldn't be super awkward or dramatic. You don't need a PowerPoint presentation or an epic monologue, just a few clear, kind words. Here are a few plug-and-play scripts to keep in your back pocket for those "uhhh... what do I say now?" moments:

For a family member who pressures you or offers "advice" that feels like control (life choices, career, dating, etc.):

"I know you mean well, but I need to make this decision on my own."

For a romantic partner, when emotions are running high, and you need a moment to gather your thoughts:

"I care about us, but I need some space to process things before we talk."

For a friend, when they want to vent but you're emotionally tapped out:

"I love being there for you, but I don't have the capacity for deep conversations today."

For work, when asked to take on more, but you're already overextended:

"I want to help, but can't commit to this without pushing past my limits."

For a parent, when they keep trying to steer your life like you're still 12:

"I respect your opinion, but I need you to trust me to live my own life."

THE BOUNDARY THAT GOT AWAY

On paper, I can talk about drawing lines in the sand all day, but I still sometimes say yes when I want to say no. I guess... that's life. The difference now? There's thought behind it. There are levels to my decision-making that feel like growth alone. If I'm mildly depleted, I'll usually go, and it's usually fine. I'm a sucker for that little voice that whispers: *Tomorrow isn't promised. Say yes. Show up for your people.*

But I have to remember: I'm "people" too. Showing up for others is a beautiful thing, but my presence loses meaning if I abandon myself in the process.

And then there are the times when I've pushed past mildly depleted and entered the completely fried zone. In those moments, I only want my bed, some snacks, and feel-good reruns. So I lie—not big ones, just small ones that keep the peace. But with each lie, I trade honesty for ease, and it adds up. Maybe they'd be fine with me saying, "I'm wiped out and need to rest," but I never gave them that chance. Instead, I served up a half-baked excuse on a paper plate of guilt.

And let's be real: lying is exhausting, plus I'm running out of fresh material. Point for Team Integrity. Zero points for my creativity. There are only so many times you can say, "I've got plans," before someone realizes the plan is just you, your remote, and a deeply committed relationship with your blankie. Avoiding honesty might save a few feelings, but it costs you peace.

Now, let's shift gears and talk about setting boundaries that reflect your values, so you don't need a script or a cover story every time. When your limits come from who you are and what matters most, saying "no" starts to feel much more natural.

1. Identify What Drains You.

What people, situations, or conversations leave you feeling depleted? That's your starting point.

2. Align with Your Values.

If peace, honesty, or growth matter, your boundaries should reflect that.

Example:

"I won't engage in gossip because I value honesty."

"I won't overcommit because I value peace and follow-through."

3. Be Clear and Direct.

"I don't think I can." → out.

"I won't be able to." → in.

4. Set Boundaries with Yourself Too.

Limit doom-scrolling, overcommitting, or saying yes out of guilt.

5. Enforce Consequences.

If someone repeatedly crosses your boundary, take action.

Example:

If a friend constantly calls late at night, tell them you won't answer after a specific time.

6. Expect Resistance.

Not everyone will love the new boundary, but that's their problem.

7. Reassess Often.

Boundaries evolve as you do.

THE COST OF PEACE IS SOMETIMES PEOPLE

Here's the part they leave out of all those "protect your peace" quotes on Pinterest: sometimes peace costs people. Yep—real, actual people. The ones who benefited from your lack of boundaries. The ones who flinch when you say no. The ones who preferred the version of you that never asked for much.

And when you start choosing yourself, not all of them stick around. It's awkward, sometimes painful, but it proves your healing is working. People who genuinely care for you won't treat your boundaries as a problem; they'll respect them and you.

Here's what often gets overlooked: boundaries may empower you, but they can also bring grief. You might lose access, closeness, or entire relationships—not because you were wrong, but because you finally told the truth about what you need. Yet in the space that loss creates, something sacred grows: peace, self-respect, room to breathe, and deeper connections that let you show up as your whole self, no edits and no apology. It's not easy, but it's the kind of hard that heals.

And remember: grieving the people who couldn't grow with you is okay. Loss is hard. Period.

No Is a Full Sentence (and a Power Move)

So now that you know what's at stake, you can start setting limits with your eyes open. You won't get it perfect every time, and you don't need to. What you *do* need is clarity and heart, the kind that keeps you grounded when saying "no" feels hard. In the words of Coach Taylor: *Clear eyes. Full hearts. Can't lose.*

Yes, Coach Taylor is fictional, but the wisdom stands. *Clear eyes* mean staying focused, seeing past fear, distractions, or guilt so you can make decisions with a clear mind. *Full hearts* mean bringing passion and courage to the table—knowing your worth, standing firm, and showing up fully. Boundaries need both. They require clear eyes to recognize what drains you, and full hearts to honor yourself enough to act on it. And of course, *can't lose* needs no explanation.

Remember, boundaries aren't about control; they're about respect. So here's your challenge: say no to anything that doesn't align with your values, energy, or peace. Even if your voice shakes, even if you need a nap and a recovery snack afterward. Set your intentions, own your space, and give it everything you've got.

Clear eyes. Real you. Let's go.

Up next: learning to keep burnout at bay through rest, reflection, and the kind of self-care that doesn't just recharge you, but actually sustains you.

Chapter 8

THE ROLE OF REST, REFLECTION, AND SELF-CARE

These days, we throw the word *self-care* around like confetti, usually alongside face masks, bubble baths, and some overpriced candle that promises to erase anxiety. But authentic self-care goes deeper than pampering. It's pausing to hear your own needs. It's reflecting on what matters. It's caring for yourself *before* you burn out, and that kind of rebellion takes practice.

At its core, self-care is about making proactive choices that protect your physical, mental, emotional, and even spiritual health. It's maintenance, not luxury. It's prevention, not recovery.

Moving your body, eating well, and getting enough rest strengthen you physically. Journaling, mindfulness, or therapy can steady your thoughts and bring clarity. Moments with loved ones or hobbies you're passionate about nurture your emotional well-being and remind you that joy is just as vital as productivity. And prevention—like regular checkups, healthy routines, and knowing your limits—helps you catch stress before it becomes exhaustion.

Of course, self-care isn't one-size-fits-all. It might look like walking in nature, reading for fun, laughing until your stomach hurts, or simply unplugging from the noise for a while. What matters most is remembering that self-care isn't optional. It's essential. When you weave it into your daily rhythm, you won't just survive the week— you might actually start to enjoy it.

SELF-CARE ISN'T JUST PRETTY... IT'S POWERFUL

Yes, I get my nails and toes done. Yes, I love a good facial and a Swedish massage. Those things make me feel fancy and amazing—like I've officially stepped into the level of bougie God always intended for me. And while I *love* that for myself, self-care goes deeper than skin. The kind that heals your mindset, restores your peace, and reconnects you to your purpose takes more effort, but it solves more problems than a lavender scented body scrub ever could.

One of the ways I've cared for my mental health is through books. *The Miracle Morning* by Hal Elrod was one of them, and it left a mark. In it, he introduces a morning routine called **SAVERS**: Silence, Affirmations, Visualization, Exercise, Reading, and Scribing (aka journaling). The idea is simple: spend a few minutes on these habits each morning to boost your growth, productivity, and overall well-being.

I was sold. Anything that can help me get my life together before breakfast deserves a shot.

Some mornings, I make it through all six. Other mornings? Not so much. Silence and visualization are the hardest for me. I sit down to meditate, and ten seconds later I'm thinking about old song lyrics, 90s sitcoms, or that one time I tripped in front of my tenth-grade crush...it's pure chaos.

Then there's visualization, where I'm trying to feel a future I've never touched, tasted, or seen. Sounds impossible, right? And yet...people swear by it. Here's how I've come to understand it: visualization isn't just wishful thinking; it's mental rehearsal. It builds belief, trains your mind for what's possible, and helps you think like the version of you already living it. I'm still wrapping my head around it, but so far, I've learned this: sometimes your mind has to see it before you do.

And these techniques aren't just good vibes and Instagram quotes; they're science-backed. Studies show that even *attempting* to meditate or visualize can boost focus, improve motivation, and shift your habits. Your brain literally primes itself to expect and notice things that align with your focus. That's your **reticular activating system (RAS)** at work—a tiny filter in your brainstem that constantly scans your environment for anything connected to what you've been dwelling on. Start visualizing peace, confidence, love, or purpose, and your RAS kicks in like an inner GPS, whispering: *This way, sis*

That said, visualizing is still work, especially when your imagination has been on a semi-permanent sabbatical. After years of just trying to keep the lights on, believing for something big feels... awkward. Especially when your subconscious keeps yelling, *Be serious. That's not for you.* Classic funhouse move.

But here's the good news: perfection isn't required. Guided or silent, chaotic or focused, even a few minutes a day can start shifting something. So give yourself permission to try, imagine, and believe. Even if your brain detours through every Maroon 5 song or some random memory from 2003, you're still doing the work.

> *"Rest isn't a prize you win, it's a gift you give yourself."*

The Power of Pausing on Purpose

I live my life by a planned, packed, and precise schedule. I run on Post-it notes, calendars, and caffeine. Asking for help? Not exactly my strong suit. I mean, the safest hands are our own, right? So I have to do everything myself...right?

Uhhh...wrong.

Here's what I've learned the hard way: if you don't sit yourself down, life will do it for you. Every time I push past my limits, my body waves the white flag with some sudden illness and forced rest. At this point, it's less of a surprise and more of a built-in feature. So now? I take the hint. Seriously, nobody needs to catch COVID for a *fourth* time.

Once I started noticing the signs (thank you, *Final Destination*), I could usually catch the crash before it hit. For example, I was working a new job (that I hated, of course), and my brain was absolutely fried. I had a vacation coming up: nine glorious days off. But before I knew it, my calendar was crammed with errands, catch-ups, and to-do lists. Seven of the nine days were already booked. Absolutely not! I canceled everything non-essential and protected those days like they were my last.

I slept. I read. I binged shows. I ignored everyone, guilt-free. And guess what? I returned refreshed and present, like a phone charged 200% after barely surviving at 1% for weeks. The job? Still trash. But that rest gave me the tools to fight for another day.

Maybe your story isn't canceling nine days of plans, but the principle's the same: sometimes you have to guard your rest like your life depends on it because, honestly, it does. Look for the signs, before life plays director and does it for you.

REST FEELS ILLEGAL...OR IS THAT JUST ME?

Even after I started honoring my need for rest, I still had moments where slowing down felt wrong. It's easy to clock out of work, but how do you rest when the sink is full of dishes, the carpet is mocking you, and the laundry pile could qualify as a federal offense? Resting felt impossible. Even on my scheduled "do-nothing" days, I was doing something. I couldn't help it. I felt guilty, like I had to earn my spot on the couch.

Then I started spending time with a guy, and by now, you should know that's never good. True to form, he was definitely not a life partner. In fact, I wish he *were* the one who got away (cue *The Civil Wars*). But he did unknowingly give me something I couldn't give myself: downtime. No appointments. No to-do list. Just naps, wine, and blessed nothingness.

When that situationship ended, I was back in my own space—busy on the surface, but hollow underneath. I wasn't just body-tired; I was soul-tired. I was craving the kind of rest sleep couldn't touch. That's when it hit me: I didn't just need time off. I needed permission to breathe, not from a partner or a planner, but from myself. So I had to retrain my mind to believe that stillness isn't lazy or indulgent. It isn't something to earn. It's necessary. Holy, even.

The Bible speaks about rest hundreds of times. In the Old Testament, it's tied to the Sabbath and God's promise of rest for His people. In the New Testament, Jesus promises rest that restores the soul.

"Come to me, all you who are weary and burdened, and I will give you rest." Matthew 11:28 (NIV)

"The Lord replied, 'My Presence will go with you, and I will give you rest.'" Exodus 33:14 (NIV)

Even God rested. As Genesis reminds us:

"By the seventh day God had finished the work he had been doing; so on the seventh day he rested from all his work." Genesis 2:2 (NIV)

So, if the Creator of the universe can take a break, how self-important am I to think I can't? Rest isn't weakness, it's worship.

RECLAIMING REST, RECLAIMING YOU

Now, I choose to rest on purpose. Not as an afterthought. Not when I'm already unraveling. I choose it as an act of self-respect. And here's the good news: you don't need a one-way ticket to Bali or a radical lifestyle overhaul to make space for rest. Simple works too.

For me, self-care often looks like:

- Listening to the rain while drinking tea.

- Curling up with my favorite book.

- Turning my phone on do not disturb.

- Watching five episodes of *Gilmore Girls* in a row (no regrets).

- Saying no when I've reached my limit.

Rest is personal. The more you practice it, the easier it is to notice what your body, mind, and spirit are asking for. And if you're not sure where to start, here's a simple check-in to guide you each week.

THE WEEKLY R.E.S.T. CHECK-IN

Reflection is rest's underrated sidekick. You can't heal what you ignore, so try this check-in once a week. Take five to ten minutes to gather your thoughts, gain insight, and return to center:

R → Run-down

Where am I feeling most physically, emotionally, or mentally drained?

E → Emotions

Have I been more irritable, anxious, or numb than usual?

S → Stillness

Did I make any space for quiet or silence this week? If not, why?

T → Time with God (or myself)

Have I taken intentional time to be still and reconnect spiritually or personally?

Bonus journaling prompt: *What would rest look and feel like for me this week?*

FOR THE MOMS WHO ARE RUNNING ON EMPTY

Even though it's not my story, I'd miss something big if I didn't pause for the moms and acknowledge that self-care looks different when raising tiny humans. I've seen how easy it is for moms to put themselves last. *When the kids are older... when school starts... when things slow down.*

Except, things don't always slow down. And your physical, mental, and emotional health isn't a luxury; it allows you to truly show up for your family. You can't pour from an empty cup, no matter how good your intentions are. At some point, you're just serving burnout with a splash of cream and calling it coffee.

Before takeoff, consider what flight attendants always say: "Put on your oxygen mask before helping others." It sounds backwards, but you can't help anyone else if you pass out. The same goes for self-care.

I've watched the women in my life juggle work, kids, home, and somehow still make cupcakes for the school fundraiser. I've also heard the loving horror stories of having to hide in the bathroom just to snag five minutes of peace. (And honestly, that door lock deserves an award.)

It may not look like a spa day or a silent retreat, but if hiding in the bathroom is the only quiet moment you get—no judgment, no shame. That still counts. It's an act of claiming space in a world that constantly asks you to give it away.

And here's the thing: you're not a snack-packing, taxi-driving, house-cleaning robot. You're a human being who deserves rest. Our bodies weren't made to live on overdrive, and chronic stress doesn't just wear you down; it can make you sick. I watched my own superwoman mom take on so much that it broke her body.

Watching that taught me something important: burnout doesn't just steal your energy. It steals your health, your joy, and precious moments with the people you love.

So, before you run yourself ragged, let's set the record straight on a few common myths:

Myth: "I don't have time."

Reality: Sometimes it feels like there's never enough, but even five minutes can make a difference. Small increments of rest still count.

Myth: "The kids come first."

Reality: Yes, they do, but you count too. They need you healthy and whole, not running on fumes.

Myth: "Self-care is selfish."

Reality: It's necessary, and it's modeling. When your kids see you set boundaries and rest, they learn it's okay to do the same.

Now, I know not every mom's situation looks the same. Some are married, some single, some "married single." Some work full-time, and some manage multiple kids of different ages. There's no one-size-fits-all solution. Still, there are a few simple ways to refuel without hitting pause on life.

Quick and Simple Self-Care Practices:

- **Try the "quiet game."** Yes, bribe them if you must... silence is golden.

- **Take a ten-minute walk, stretch, or sneak in "bite-sized workouts."** Small movements can reset your mood.

- **Take a few deep breaths.** It may not feel like much, but it's a quiet power move you can pull out whenever needed.

- **Take care of your appearance,** whether it's a haircut or just putting on an outfit that makes you feel human again.

- **Schedule tiny "me time" appointments.** A hot shower, a chapter of your book, or coffee in peace can go a long way.

- **Nap when they nap.** The dishes won't wash themselves, but they'll still be there later. Refilling your tank is more important than an empty sink.

Beyond the quick resets, your everyday habits matter just as much. Eat something nourishing that isn't your kid's leftover mac and cheese, and don't forget to hydrate (coffee doesn't count, I checked). Guard your sleep; revenge scrolling will betray you every time. And take a second to jot down one thing you're grateful for, even if it's just *"nobody spilled anything today."*

And don't do it alone. Ask for help and say yes when it's offered. Spend time with other adults so you don't forget how to form complete sentences. Let go of the idea that saying "no" makes you a bad mom; it makes you wise.

The bottom line is that self-care is maintenance for your body and soul. It's choosing to be human, not superhuman. When you're healthy, rested, and grounded, your family is stronger too. You deserve that now, not someday. Oxygen mask on first, mama.

REST LIKE YOU MEAN IT

Ultimately, whether you're juggling kids, careers, or just your own expectations, the principle is the same: you can't thrive without rest. Self-care gives you the tools to rebuild when life wears you down. It's the quiet declaration that says, "I'm worth showing up for." So whether it's a nap, a walk, a guided meditation, or simply saying "no" to one more obligation...take the time. Reclaim your peace. Return to the calm place inside where your soul can finally exhale. Rest isn't a perk or a prize; it's a requirement.

Up next: The people around you matter more than you think. Let's talk about what happens when your circle is part of your healing or part of your hurt.

Chapter 9

SURROUNDING YOURSELF WITH SUPPORT

The people around you matter more than you think. Friends, family, coworkers, and even messy entanglements shape how you see yourself. Healthy relationships are anchors. They steady you when you tremble, hold space when you feel small, and breathe life into your weary soul. They remind you that you are seen, valued, and loved.

Toxic relationships, though, are distortions in disguise. They twist how you see yourself until you barely recognize who you've become. They drain you, warp your peace, and mold you into someone you were never meant to be. And somewhere along the way, you forget what safe even feels like.

CHOSEN, BUT NOT CHERISHED

Speaking of toxic, let's head back to my junior year, when I caught feelings for one of the star athletes. You might remember my charming high school boyfriend, known for his love of body-shaming. At first, he was just this cute, popular guy, and for reasons I (and most of the girls in my class) couldn't understand, he picked me. Plain ol' me. No makeup, oversized jackets, sneakers, and a unibrow. I know I'm painting quite the picture, but I promise I was cute—just not *star-athlete* cute.

So, for him to choose me? It felt amazing. I felt seen, like I'd won something. Boy, was I wrong.

A few years in, I realized something... he never complimented me. Not once. So, one day, I asked if he thought I was pretty. His response? "I'm with you, aren't I?"

I was stunned! The way I stood there blinking, you'd think I was silently solving for X. Eventually, my brain rebooted, and I asked, "So...you *do* think I'm pretty?" And he said... nothing. Just stood there munching on chips, looking confused about *my* confusion as if *I* were the one making it weird.

At 18, I didn't know what to do with that. Obviously, he must've found me attractive if he was with me. But emotionally, that pause said something different and planted a seed: *You don't measure up, so just be grateful you have someone.* So I stayed. I endured. And after eight long years, I was finally set free. But how many more seeds had been planted by then? Seeds of insecurity, teaching me to settle for scraps. Seeds of false loyalty, convincing me that endurance was love. Little lies that grew roots so deep I lost sight of what love truly was.

It took years to rewire that part of my brain. Eventually, I learned that wanting someone in your life doesn't mean they deserve to be there. Hanging on isn't loyalty, it's self-harm, because some people leave marks that don't fade. Thinking back on those years pushed me to start taking inventory of my circle: who was pouring into me, and who was bleeding me dry?

That's what led me to a simple but eye-opening exercise I call...

THE WHO'S WHO

I've done my people audit; now it's your turn. Grab a pen.
Take a breath. Ask the hard questions: Who makes you feel safe,
supported, and seen? Who leaves you second-guessing everything
you say and everything you are? The people around you shape your
reflection, whether you notice it or not. So, are you ready to face
it?

Here's what to do: make two lists. They can be side by side in
columns, on separate pages, in your journal, or even in the notes
app on your phone. Write their names. Note what they add to your
life or what they take away. Here are some signs:

Uplifters

- Offer encouragement without guilt

- Respect your boundaries

- Speak the truth with kindness

- Leave you feeling energized

- Make hard conversations feel safe

Drainers

- Constantly criticize or compare

- Make everything about them

- Guilt-trip you for setting boundaries

- Leave you feeling small, guilty, or exhausted

- Bring chaos, not calm

Now that you've got your list, review it. Who's adding to your peace, and who's chipping away at it? You don't have to cut everyone off tomorrow. But this is your starting point, the moment you sharpen your scissors and start protect your peace.

> *"You weren't meant to walk alone, but not every hand deserves to hold yours."*

PUT IT ON PAPER, WATCH IT GET REAL

Sure, you could have done this audit in your head, but putting it on paper makes the impact real.

When thoughts stay in your mind, they remain jumbled and overwhelming. But once they're on the page, you can't ignore them anymore. Your brain slows down, sorts through the noise, and starts making sense of things. You move from reacting to processing, spiraling to sorting, from feeling stuck to finally seeing what's happening.

Writing it down also makes it undeniable. No more gaslighting yourself with *"maybe I'm overthinking"* because now you can see and examine it. And when it's painful, putting it on paper gives you both compassion and distance. It's like reminding yourself: *This is a chapter, not the whole book.* You stop living inside the chaos and start observing it.

On the page, it becomes more than words; it becomes a cue to guard your peace, even when your emotions wage war against it.

BARE-FACED AND GLOWING

Enough about the drainers. Let's talk about the beautiful people who uplift, steady, and remind you that you're not alone—the ones who see the mess and show up anyway. They call you back to your worth, not because you're perfect, but because you're *you*. This kind of support reinforces the truth that you deserve love, even in your messiest moments. You can ask for help and still be strong. You can lean on someone without losing yourself.

That's why the people around you matter. The right ones don't just cheer you on; they pour strength back into you when you're running on empty. And I've experienced that firsthand...

One day, I was telling one of my close friends, who's basically a walking, talking fashion editorial, how much I admired her style and wished I could be that girl: the naturally stylish diva who always serves a look. Her response stopped me in my tracks: *"You are effortlessly beautiful with a wonderful personality. You don't need anything more, and I need you to internalize that."*

I almost cried. (Okay, I did cry but only on the inside.) I wish I could say that moment instantly changed me, but it didn't. What it did do was start to uproot some of the weeds planted years earlier by my boyfriend—and that pause, the one that etched insecurity into my bones. As I learned more about reframing, the narrative started to shift. I went from:

- From *plain* → *natural.*

- From *awkward* → *authentic.*

- From *invisible* → *radiant.*

There will always be people who prefer makeup, glam, or high fashion, and that's okay. But there's also nothing wrong with being someone who feels beautiful bare-faced.

Natural beauty is a flex. Not because it's "better," but because I've grown enough to feel at home in my own skin. I can stand next to the divas in my life and know my light shines just as bright.

My friend (and a few others) helped me stand firm in my truth. They continue to uplift me, reminding me that the gift wrap is cute, but what's inside matters most. That's the kind of love that heals. The kind that doesn't try to fix you but simply sits beside you and holds your hand. And once you've experienced that kind of love, it's much easier to spot the unhealthy kind.

RED LIGHT, GREEN LIGHT, 1-2-3

Easier doesn't mean easy. Unhealthy relationships don't come with warning sirens and red tape. Sometimes they look charming, helpful, even loving, and you don't realize there's a problem until your peace leaks away little by little. You'll find yourself over-explaining, second-guessing, and walking on eggshells to "keep the peace," while your nervous system quietly screams, *Something's not right.* Listen to that, it often knows before your brain catches up.

Red Flag (aka Your Soul's Alarm System):

- Constant criticism or passive-aggressive jabs

- One-sided effort that leaves you feeling drained or resentful

- Gaslighting, blame-shifting, or making you feel "too sensitive"

- Love or approval that feels earned instead of given

- Dismissed boundaries, guilt-trips, or silent treatment

Green Flag (aka Peace You Can Feel):

- Kindness that's consistent, not performative or conditional

- Open, honest communication even when it's uncomfortable

- Respect for your space, your pace, and your *no*

- Disagreements that don't lead to punishment or shame

- Accountability, apologies that come with change, and a willingness to grow

Safe relationships aren't perfect, but they're honest. They make room for your voice, your needs, and your healing. After enough toxic ones, safety can feel boring at first, but it's not. It's unfamiliar until you realize it's the standard you deserve.

LEFT ON READ, LED BY GOD

Let's break up the heavy and talk about the one time I shot my shot. There was a guy at my job who was very swoon-worthy. After I quit, I texted him to say I was interested, and... crickets. Not a "thanks," not a "sorry," not even an emoji. I wanted to disappear.

But months later, I found out he plays for Team Toxic. This guy wouldn't have been a pleasant addition to my life and would've undone all the work I'd put into getting my circle right. That moment didn't just teach me about rejection, because it was more than that. I realize now it was a block... a divine one.

If you're a person of faith like me, you understand: sometimes God blocks what we ask for to protect us. He has a way of keeping your peace intact, even when it stings. Though personally, I'd appreciate Him throwing the block *before* I hit send.

WITH A PINCH OF DISCERNMENT

Stories like that highlight that getting caught up in the magic is easy, even when you know better, which is why you also need spiritual wisdom when auditioning for your circle. When walking with God, discernment and prayer help you filter the hype. They slow you down long enough to ask: *Is this person pulling me closer to who I'm becoming or dragging me back into who I'm trying to heal from?*

God may not answer with lightning bolts, but He does nudge. That *"something's off"* feeling? The unease you can't shake, gently whispering, "Molly, you in danger, girl." Pay attention to that. Before I knew God, I called it intuition—a gut feeling that nudged me away from certain people or toward unexpected choices. I didn't have the words for it, but I knew something was guiding me.

After I met God, I realized that "something" had a name: the Holy Spirit. It's not some vague feeling, but the very presence of God within me providing divine direction. So now when I hear the whisper, I know who's behind it. Discernment doesn't have to be loud to lead you to the truth.

If you're unsure whether someone's presence is healthy, don't just listen to their words; look at their fruit. Not apples and oranges, but the fruit of their spirit—what Paul lists in Galatians: love, joy, peace, patience, kindness, goodness, faithfulness, gentleness, and self-control. That's not just a checklist. It's the evidence of God's Spirit at work. If someone consistently brings chaos instead of peace, control instead of gentleness, guilt instead of love, that's not just a red flag. That's divine discernment waving a flashlight in your face.

HEALING MEANS BEING CHOOSY

Once you learn the language of your soul—your rhythms, your wounds, your why—you stop letting empty company wander into sacred spaces. You no longer say yes just to quiet the loneliness. Instead, you start choosing:

- Connection over chaos

- Clarity over confusion

- Respect over attention

- Love over love-bombing

It's not about being a diva. It's about knowing your value and choosing accordingly. I recently came across this quote: "Normalize choosing standards over desperation, and freedom over fake fairy tales. Because a ring without respect is a handcuff in disguise."

While I believe in being choosy in every relationship, not just the romantic ones, I've got to give that line its flowers. It deserves respect, applause, a Grammy, a TED Talk, and honestly? Its own merch line.

All jokes aside, the truth underneath that quote is this: real connection comes from relationships that bring peace and freedom. Standards protect your worth, and choosing them means honoring your value enough to wait for what truly aligns with you.

So here's the challenge: choose people who value the you you're becoming, not just the one you've been. People who bring peace, not confusion. Growth, not games. People who remind you that you're already enough.

And a quick note for anyone who doesn't yet have a tribe: I believe healthy relationships can be anchors—the kind that steady you and keep you grounded—but there may be times when you won't have one to hold onto. If that's the season you're in, take heart. As Mama McCall wisely said in *Teen Wolf:* "Be your own anchor." I take that to mean stand strong. Don't settle for less just to fill the silence. Trust that God is preparing the right people for you, in His timing. Your tribe is coming, handpicked and heaven-sent.

Up next: what if your confidence isn't gone, just buried under years of doubt, fear, and other people's projections? Let's talk about how to uncover it.

Chapter 10

MOVING FORWARD WITH PURPOSE & PERSISTENCE

Let's be honest, persistence sounds noble in theory. But it doesn't just live in big victories. It can look like showing up when you'd rather hide, holding on in a relationship that feels impossible, or forcing yourself to push through a job that drains the life out of you. I've experienced all of those kinds of persistence.

For me, it was the jobs that pushed me to the brink, leaving me exhausted and questioning all my life choices. Every day blurred into the next. I'd come home too tired to cook, too drained to think, and too numb to care. I thought structure and stability would fix it.

Have you ever dreamt of that magical 9-to-5, Monday-to-Friday office life? I did. So I left my physically exhausting part-time job for the "grown-up" full-time cubicle life I just knew was an upgrade. Yeah... turns out, not so much.

By year two, I was juggling over a hundred cases across four programs. I was still learning the ropes, barely breathing, yet the powers that be expected me to deliver like a seasoned pro. As if that wasn't hard enough, all of this happened during a global pandemic, when the world felt chaotic and strangely apocalyptic. I was just trying to stay afloat while the world was on fire—but I was one case away from combusting. It was exhausting. It was madness. It was misery.

So why didn't I quit? Simple: I had responsibilities, a mother to care for, and, of course, *bills, bills, bills* (cue Destiny's Child). But underneath it all was fear. I was afraid I wouldn't find anything better. I was afraid I'd have to exchange PTO, pay, or retirement for freedom. So I stayed. I fought. I built a system of sticks, glue, hopes, and prayers. It wasn't perfect, but it kept me afloat as long as I was never sick, never late, and never took a vacation.

As it turns out, my system wasn't exactly sustainable, so I bolted when I saw an opening. I transferred to another department with the same pension, same PTO, no caseload, and slightly fewer headaches. Still, I wouldn't call it thriving, but I was surviving. And sometimes, that's all you get.

THE ULTIMATE TRUST FALL

Persistence can get you through the hardest seasons, but without purpose, you can end up just getting by instead of truly living. That's where faith comes in. Purpose gives your steps direction, but faith gives them strength.

Moving with purpose doesn't just take discipline or strategy. It asks for trust: knowing when to stand still and when to step out. Not every decision comes with guarantees, and that's where faith meets forward motion.

I began to understand this more when I noticed how faith had been quietly working around me, long before I could name it. For example, when my cousin mailed my mom a check for the exact amount she had been praying for, or when we had no money for food and, instead of calling anyone, my mom said, "I'm only calling Jesus." A few hours later, my aunt showed up with groceries.

Again and again, small moments reminded me that God was real and that faith meant moving forward without proof. So when I finally walked away from the "no-caseload-but-still-soul-crushing" full-time job and into a part-time gig that barely covered rent, people thought I'd lost it. But deep down, I knew I wouldn't fall, and I didn't.

That decision taught me persistence doesn't always mean hustling harder; sometimes, it means relaxing and trusting the process, even when the outcome is unclear. It was the first time I trusted something bigger than my fear, and it changed everything. It showed me that moving forward with purpose takes courage. Choosing to step out on faith again and again—that's persistence wrapped in faith.

THE SOUNDTRACK OF SURVIVAL

Not every hard thing is meant to be endured. Sticking with something challenging only matters when it's leading you somewhere better. That kind of persistence builds grit and self-trust. Whether it's love, work, or life, it all counts. You realize you're stronger than you thought when you keep showing up. You can face discomfort and still move forward.

Sometimes persistence shows up like a movie moment—tears in your eyes, music swelling, the whole cinematic comeback. Other times, it's subtle, like turning on the computer when you'd rather throw it or dragging yourself out the door with your pick-me-up playlist blasting on repeat.

That was me. When life rocked me, I went searching for musical motivation to keep on keeping on. *Carry On Wayward Son* carried me out of more than one mess. And if you don't have a go-to song that lifts you up when you can't lift yourself, get one.

And it's not just my theory, science says so. Music can lift your mood, trick your brain into feeling less tired, and push you to keep going when you'd rather quit. For me, *Carry On* was more than background noise; it reminded me that battles unseen are still battles fought. And as any *Supernatural* fan knows, that song hits different when you're barely holding it together. *Carry On* isn't just a lyric, it's a promise. A defiant kind of hope. A soundtrack to survival.

(Cue dramatic montage: dusky highway, Dean at the wheel, healing in the passenger seat... and me in the middle, obviously.)

Unfortunately, some storylines drag on with no season finale in sight, and sometimes you need more than a musical anthem to make it through. That's when you have to give yourself grace—especially when your endurance runs low and the plot twists won't stop. Never forget, you're still the main character. You're still here, still breathing, still writing the story, still carrying on.

And in case no one's told you lately, allow me: persistence isn't about being fearless or flawless. It's the decision to steady yourself and take the next brave step, even if you're out of steam, running only on caffeine and prayers.

The reward for resilience doesn't show up immediately; sometimes, the lesson comes first. And sometimes that lesson is all you get—but if you're lucky, it's the blessing you need. I learned that firsthand through my job struggles. Remember that cubicle life I thought would be my upgrade? Yeah, it was not giving what it needed to give, but it stretched me. That season proved I could handle more than I thought.

It also made me see my exhaustion wasn't just about work; it was about living a life that didn't fit me. Alone with my thoughts during an endless 12-hour shift in a windowless room, I finally asked: *What do I really want? Who do I want to be? Why do I keep ignoring the nudge that maybe... just maybe... I was made for more?* To my surprise, that period of reflection helped lead me to school and later to this book. Life is sneaky like that.

FAIL FORWARD, BABE

Here's the danger of persistence: sometimes you take a big fat L, and I'm sure we can all agree—it sucks. Failure feels like a punch to the gut. Rejection stings. Setbacks disappoint. But none of that makes you a failure. You're trying. You're growing. The more you learn to embrace these moments, the more confident and resilient you become. You stop seeing failure as an identity and start seeing it as a lesson in disguise, an invitation to pivot, and proof of bravery.

Failure isn't the end of your story; it's a comma, not a period. It's a plot twist that may not feel good, but it might set you up for something better. Need a little proof? There are plenty of people who stumbled before they soared. Sometimes the most iconic journeys begin with a detour.

- **Oprah Winfrey**–Told she was "too emotionally invested" for TV.

- **Steve Jobs**–Fired from Apple, the company he co-founded.

- **J. K. Rowling**–Rejected by 12 publishers before *Harry Potter* changed the world.

- **Michael Jordan**–Cut from his high school basketball team.

- **Thomas Edison**–1,000+ failed attempts before the lightbulb.

- **Walt Disney**–Fired for "lacking imagination."

- **Colonel Sanders**–Rejected over 1,000 times before someone said yes to his chicken...at age 62.

What do they all have in common? They failed forward. They didn't quit. So maybe failure isn't a stop sign. It's a slingshot pulling you back far enough to launch you into what's next.

To borrow my favorite quote: "Sometimes, the beauty is in the attempt." Not in the result, the applause, or the perfect storyline—just the fact that you tried. You showed up with your heart in your hand, and that matters.

> *"Healing is messy. Growth is slow. But you're still moving, and that counts."*

WHEN LIFE SAYS "NOPE," SAY "NOTED"

Now, let's welcome back an old friend: *reframing*. It's the tool that takes the sting of failure and flips it into something that builds you instead of breaking you. Reframing isn't pretending things are fine; it's choosing not to camp out in shame, regret, or defeat. It's how you shift your perspective to move forward with clarity (and maybe even a little peace).

If you're looking for reframing examples, start here:

1. See Failure as Feedback

Failure isn't a final grade; it's a note in the margin that says, "Try this instead." Every misstep gives you data on what worked, what didn't, and how to improve it.

2. Focus on What You Learned

It's easy to focus on what went wrong, but pause and ask: What did I gain? Insight? Toughness? Clarity? Growth often hides in the rubble.

3. Recognize That Everyone Fails

You're not the exception; you're the rule. Every successful person has a trail of flops behind them. You know the motto: fall down seven times, get up eight.

4. Shift From "I Failed" to "I'm Still Learning"

Words matter. Some keep you stuck, others keep you moving; you're not a failure but a learner in motion.

5. Celebrate the Effort

Showing up, trying again, and asking for help. Wins don't measure courage; it's measured by your willingness to try when there are no guarantees.

6. Use It as Motivation

Let the frustration fuel you, not in a "prove them wrong" way (unless that helps), but in a "I'm not done yet" way. Let the pain have a purpose.

Failure doesn't get the last word unless you stop moving. So don't. Keep learning, keep showing up, and keep rewriting the story. Sometimes the messiest chapters lead to the best plot twists.

TERRIFIED BUT TYPING

Remember when I told you I have a paralyzing fear of failure? Well, this book is my walking-with-fear moment, live and in blazing color.

What if no one reads it?

What if people think it's stupid?

What if they're right?

These thoughts play on a loop because, where I come from, writing books was never on anybody's radar. This is outside the norm. We're not artists—we're grinders. We show up to jobs we don't love and do what we must. We don't make things; we make it work. And yet, here I am, typing away.

A quote I love popped up on my social media feed a while back: "Feel the fear and do it anyway." It hit me so hard, I made it my Facebook cover photo. (Yes, I'm dating myself, but at least I didn't say Myspace... oops.) It stuck with me because it didn't ask me to be fearless; it invited me to move with the fear. To listen to the tiny voice whispering, *but... what if? What if this helps someone? What if I was made for this?*

Jim Rohn said it best: "Why not you? Why not now?" So no, I have no idea how all this will turn out. And yes, I'm still nervous. But I was created for more than fear, and so were you. Chances are, you've got your own "what if" moment tugging at your heart. So here's the deal: I'll keep showing up scared, if you will.

LET GRACE SET THE PACE

Our culture loves to glamorize hustle culture and #teamnosleep, but honestly? Hard pass. Yes, get things done, but rest is not the enemy of resilience. You can move forward without sprinting. You can be driven and still be led. Let peace, not panic, be your compass. The persistence born from peace is the kind that endures because grace walks with it. And while peace may not always look like progress, it's where you return to your most authentic self.

So here's what I hope you remember: failure is not your identity, rejection is not your worth, fear is not a stop sign, and loving yourself completely isn't required to begin. Even if it's slow or no one claps for you, you're still moving forward. The cracks don't need repairing; they're part of your story—the very places where strength takes root.

Up next: A final reminder that this journey isn't about being someone else. It's about coming home to who you've always been. One last chapter, one big exhale. Let's wrap this up right, because you made it.

Conclusion

BECOMING WHO YOU WERE MEANT TO BE

Here we are, the final chapter. But spoiler alert: my journey's still unfolding, and so is yours. Building self-worth isn't a finish line with confetti and instant clarity (though wouldn't that be nice?). It's a lifelong process, a daily practice. Painful at times, but worth it. You won't feel flawless every day. Some days you slay; other days, you barely make it out of bed. That's life. The goal isn't to feel confident 24/7. It's to stop abandoning yourself on the days you don't.

MEASURING UP TO WHAT?

I spent so long chasing "enough" that I couldn't see what was already there. I used to think my value would arrive with the title, the success, the name placard, the polished "after" photo. But as that version of success kept slipping further away, I started to spiral, wondering why I was failing at life. Turns out, I wasn't. My story was just missing some vital info.

You don't earn self-worth by proving anything; you build it by getting to know the real you. So what do I know about me? I am one of one. No one else has my laugh, my voice, my perspective; they're all custom-made. When God created me, He threw away the mold. So no, I don't need a title, a ring, a degree, or anyone's approval to feel valuable. My worth was never up for debate, and neither is yours.

As Tyrese once said (yes, that Tyrese): "I love me, independent of you loving me. And if you stop loving me, I'm not gonna love myself any less." Whew... that's the type of line that hits you where you live. It made me realize how many years I spent waiting for validation, waiting for someone to love me so I could feel worthy of it, waiting for some man to call me beautiful so I could finally believe it, too.

I know I'm not alone. How many of us still wait for someone else to tell us what we're worth? Enough of that. Validation begins within, and once you truly internalize that truth, you stop panicking when someone doesn't "get" you. Turns out, I'm not for everyone, and that's okay. It's not a flaw; it's a filter, one I've learned to be grateful for because it saves me from being cast in roles I was never meant to play.

It took me a long time to think differently because validation is intoxicating. But once I stopped chasing approval, everything became clearer. Let this be your reminder that your worth begins with you.

- Your value doesn't vanish because someone else couldn't see it.

- Your realness is your power. Stop shrinking for spaces that can't hold you.

- If someone thinks you're too much, tell them to go find less.

- Finding your way doesn't start with a map; it starts with a mirror.

- You're worthy even in progress; shine while under construction.

BECOMING IN PROGRESS

It's hard watching everyone be ten steps ahead—traveling, buying houses, launching businesses, falling in love—while you're barely holding it together. Social media makes it look like everyone else has their act together, meanwhile, you're trying not to cry into your mimosa at brunch. But stuck doesn't mean something's wrong with you; sometimes it simply means you're in the self-discovery chapter of your story.

Who you are is not a flaw to fix; it's the foundation. How you think, speak, feel, and dream isn't "too much" or "not enough." It's your superpower. The world doesn't need more polished replicas. It needs your quiet strength, awkward humor, loud laugh, and messy middle. You weren't made to shrink. You were made to unfold with purpose, in your own time.

> *"If your heart's still beating, your story's not done."*

NOT FINISHED, BUT FIERCE

I'm still a work in progress, far from polished, still growing, still healing. But I've come far enough to know that having it all figured out isn't required to be proud of how far you've come. Wear your under-construction sign like a badge of honor. Show up with your scrapes, scars, setbacks, and strengths. Remember, every test you've endured is a testimony of God's grace. So tell your story; it's powerful and still being written.

Make a vow to be five percent more honest, five percent more bold, five percent more *you*. Listen to yourself, not the voice of fear. Say no when you mean no. Rest when you're tired. Write the thing. Speak up. Choose you, even when it's uncomfortable.

You don't have to flip your whole life upside down. All it takes is one small step in a new direction. Becoming is built into those everyday choices not to walk away from yourself. Each step may feel small, but together they become a path, a pattern, a promise. Nothing changes if nothing changes, so change something, and let that spark be the first light breaking through the cracks.

FINAL MIRROR MOMENT

Clarity begins with you, so before you go, ask yourself: What version of you started this journey, and more importantly, who's walking out of it? Be honest and be proud, because even if you're still figuring it out, you've already come further than you think.

Hold your head high, take a breath, and keep going. The distorted mirror has told your story for too long, but you shattered it, burned down the tent, and walked out of the funhouse and into the light.

Your shattered reflection isn't your downfall; it's your unveiling.

Note from the Author

Thank you for being here. I'm truly grateful. If something in these pages spoke to you—if it made you laugh, nod along, or dramatically reevaluate your life—that's the icing on the cake. This story may have begun with me, but it continues with you. And like a certain childhood favorite reminds us, the best stories never really end, they keep unfolding in new hands, as long as someone dares to believe.

Now, I need to ask you for a favor. Could you leave a review? I'm a first-time, self-published author, so there's no big marketing team behind me. It's just me, some hope, and a lot of prayers, so your review isn't just helpful—it's life-giving, like the iced coffee of the book world.

Stay Connected

If you're craving a peaceful space to reflect, grow, and reconnect with purpose, you'll find it in my cozy corner on **Substack:** taliespeaks.substack.com.

Bonus

A Little Something for the Road

This book isn't a quick fling; it's here for the long haul. I poured my heart into these pages, hoping to leave words that echo when you need them most. *Scattered* is the friend you can be honest with—the voice that whispers, "keep going" when you're ready to quit. It was designed to move in, shift the furniture, and take up permanent space in your everyday life.

And while these pages can offer truth, the real work happens when you start living it. The real magic shows up when you pause to reflect, challenge your patterns, and actually do something different.

One of the simplest ways to start? Give your inner struggles a name, because what you can name, you can face. I call it the Funhouse Mirror because it's where my critic performs. You can adopt that name or come up with something over-the-top like "Captain Distortion," "Drama Queen Deluxe," or anything that helps you laugh at the act instead of believing it.

Whatever you call it, just remember that voice isn't you. Every time you challenge the lies, you're shattering another warped reflection that never clearly showed you in the first place. Growth is often subtle, but whenever you choose yourself, speak kindly to yourself, or show up with a little more self-respect than yesterday, that's a win.

Here's a quick starter pack to help you keep going:

JOURNAL PROMPTS FOR REFLECTION

1. When do I feel most confident, and what am I doing in those moments?

2. What negative beliefs about myself have I carried from my past, and are they true?

3. What's one thing I've accomplished that I didn't believe I could? What does that tell me about my potential?

SAMPLE AFFIRMATIONS

Say them aloud. Write them down. Whisper them if you must, but don't stop.

- I am worthy of love, respect, and kindness.

- My past does not define me.

- I choose to see myself through the lens of love and compassion.

REAL-LIFE APPLICATION

- Catch your inner critic. Reframe the message. Call out the lie.

- Celebrate your progress; setbacks don't erase growth.

- Give yourself grace. You're allowed to take your time.

If these exercises sparked something in you, don't stop here. The *Shattered Reflections Workbook* takes it further, with 40+ practical exercises, reflection prompts, and affirmations designed to carry these truths into your everyday life.

FINAL THOUGHTS

This is your life. Your story. You are Batman, not Robin. So, take what you've learned, run with it, and make it yours. Let it show up in muddled moments, silent mornings, awkward conversations, breakthrough prayers, and late-night pep talks. Because in all those moments, you are capable, worthy, and deserve a life that reflects your values, voice, and vision.

You've already come so far, and that is proof that you can keep going. Now go out there and live like it. Boldly and without apology. You've got this.

About the author

Talie Rowe writes with honesty, humor, and heart about the journey to becoming who you were always meant to be. A Bay Area native fueled by coffee and sarcasm, she grew up asking too many questions, collecting too many knickknacks, and trying on too many versions of herself before realizing the reflection in the mirror wasn't the whole story.

Having spent years navigating self-doubt and awkward detours, Talie now writes for anyone who has ever felt stuck, unseen, or not enough. Through her words, she hopes readers find the same grace, clarity, and courage that carried her through seasons of doubt.

When she isn't writing, Talie can usually be found baking something sweet, spending time with family, or curled up with her favorite shows. *Shattered Reflections* is her debut book.

You can learn more at:
JourneyBegins.net
YouTube: Talie Speaks
Instagram: @TalieSpeaks

www.ingramcontent.com/pod-product-compliance
Lightning Source LLC
LaVergne TN
LVHW041323080426
835513LV00008B/566